Pionus Parrot

Handbook

A Detailed Guide to Pionus Parrot Care, Training, Diet and Health for Beginners and Experts - Everything You Need to Know About Owning, Breeding and Keeping Pionus Parrots as Pets

Niesha M. Sherman

Table of Contents

Introduction

Pionus parrots, known for their captivating personalities and vibrant plumage, are a beloved choice for avian enthusiasts. With their gentle demeanor, moderate size, and relatively low noise levels compared to other parrot species, Pionus parrots make ideal pets for both novice and experienced bird owners. This comprehensive guide aims to provide a detailed exploration of Pionus parrot care, from understanding their unique characteristics and selecting the right bird to mastering advanced training techniques and addressing the specific needs of breeding or senior parrots.

Raising and keeping Pionus parrots involves a multifaceted approach that encompasses proper nutrition, veterinary care, environmental enrichment, and social interaction. Each stage of a parrot's life, from hatchling to senior, presents distinct challenges and opportunities for fostering a healthy, happy, and well-adjusted companion.

This guide is structured to offer a thorough understanding of what it takes to provide optimal care for Pionus parrots. Starting with an overview of the species and their natural history, we will delve into the specifics of selecting and preparing for a Pionus parrot, creating a suitable living environment, and meeting their dietary needs. Further sections will cover health maintenance, behavioral training, and the special considerations required for breeding pairs and aging birds.

Whether you are a prospective owner seeking to learn about the basics of Pionus parrot care or an experienced handler looking to deepen your knowledge and skills, this guide is designed to equip you with the essential information and practical advice needed to ensure your parrot thrives. By understanding and meeting the diverse needs of Pionus parrots, you can build a rewarding and lasting relationship with these delightful avian companions.

CHAPTER ONE

Introduction to Pionus Parrots

1.1 What are Pionus Parrots?

Pionus parrots are a group of medium-sized parrots native to Central and South America, known for their calm demeanor, unique physical characteristics, and vibrant personalities. They belong to the genus Pionus within the family Psittacidae, which encompasses a variety of parrot species.

Fig 1: Pionus Parrots

Physical Characteristics

Pionus parrots are generally medium-sized, with most species measuring between 10 to 12 inches (25 to 30 cm) in length and weighing around 200 to 300 grams. They have a robust build with a short, square tail and a relatively large head. One of their distinguishing features is the presence of a bare, fleshy ring around the eyes, known as the eye ring, which can be a different color than the feathers surrounding it. This feature is particularly noticeable and can help in identifying specific species within the genus.

Their plumage is predominantly green, but they also exhibit a range of other colors depending on the species. For instance, the Blue-headed Pionus (Pionus menstruus) is noted for its striking blue head, while the White-crowned Pionus (Pionus senilis) has a distinctive white crown. Many species also display vibrant colors on their under-tail coverts, often in shades of red, blue, or violet.

Temperament and Behavior

Pionus parrots are often praised for their calm and gentle nature compared to other parrot species. They tend to be less noisy and less demanding, making them suitable pets for people who prefer a quieter bird. Despite their generally calm demeanor, Pionus parrots are also known to be curious and playful, enjoying a variety of toys and activities to keep them engaged.

These parrots are relatively easy to socialize and can form strong bonds with their owners. They may not be as cuddly as some other parrot species, but they enjoy interacting with humans and can become quite affectionate once a bond is established. Pionus parrots are also known for their ability to mimic sounds and human speech, although they are not as prolific talkers as some of the larger parrot species like African Greys or Amazons.

Lifespan and Health

Pionus parrots have a relatively long lifespan, often living 25 to 40 years with proper care. This longevity means that potential owners should be prepared for a long-term commitment. Regular veterinary check-ups, a balanced diet, and a stimulating environment are crucial for maintaining the health and well-being of these parrots.

Common health issues in Pionus parrots include respiratory problems, feather plucking, and obesity. Regular interaction and observation can help in early detection and prevention of these health problems. A diet rich in fruits, vegetables, and high-quality pellets, along with regular exercise, is essential for their overall health.

Habitat and Natural Environment

In the wild, Pionus parrots are found in a variety of habitats ranging from lowland rainforests to mountainous regions. They are native to a broad range that extends from Mexico through Central America and into South America. These parrots are typically found in small flocks and are known for their strong flying abilities. They feed on a diverse diet that includes fruits, seeds, nuts, berries, and occasional insects.

Their natural behaviors include foraging, climbing, and socializing with other members of their flock. These behaviors should be encouraged and facilitated in captivity to ensure their physical and mental well-being. Providing a variety of toys, foraging opportunities, and a spacious cage can help mimic their natural environment and keep them stimulated.

Importance in Aviculture

Pionus parrots are highly regarded in aviculture due to their manageable size, pleasant temperament, and relative ease of care compared to some other parrot species. They are suitable for both novice and experienced bird keepers. The relatively low noise level and their ability to adapt to different living situations make them a popular choice for people living in apartments or houses.

Pionus parrots are a captivating and rewarding species for those interested in keeping parrots as pets. Their unique combination of physical beauty, gentle temperament, and engaging personality makes them an excellent choice for bird enthusiasts. Understanding the basic characteristics and needs of Pionus parrots is the first step in ensuring a successful and fulfilling relationship with these wonderful birds.

1.2 History and Background of Pionus Parrots

Pionus parrots are indigenous to Central and South America, with their range extending from Mexico through Panama and into South America, including countries like Colombia, Venezuela, Brazil, and Peru. These parrots inhabit a variety of ecosystems, ranging from tropical lowland forests to mountainous regions, demonstrating their adaptability to diverse environmental conditions.

Historical Discovery and Taxonomy

The history of Pionus parrots in scientific literature dates back to the 18th and 19th centuries when European explorers and naturalists began documenting the flora and fauna of the New World. The genus Pionus was first described by German naturalist Johann Georg Wagler in 1832. The name "Pionus" is derived from the Greek word "pionos," meaning "fat" or "plump," likely referring to the robust body shape of these parrots.

The taxonomy of Pionus parrots has undergone several revisions as ornithologists have studied their physical characteristics, vocalizations, and genetic makeup. Today, the genus comprises several recognized species, each with distinct features and behaviors.

Cultural and Historical Significance

Pionus parrots have been part of indigenous cultures in Central and South America for centuries. Native tribes often revered these birds for their vibrant plumage and engaging personalities. Feathers from Pionus parrots were used in traditional clothing and ceremonial headdresses.

During the colonial era, Pionus parrots caught the attention of European explorers and traders. Their relatively calm demeanor and striking appearance made them popular among collectors and bird enthusiasts. This led to the exportation of these parrots to Europe, where they became part of avicultural collections and private menageries.

Introduction to Aviculture

The introduction of Pionus parrots into aviculture began in earnest during the 19th century. As European interest in exotic birds grew, these parrots became more commonly imported and bred in captivity. Early aviculturists appreciated the Pionus parrots for their manageable size, striking colors, and relatively quiet nature compared to other parrot species.

Breeding programs were established to ensure the sustainability of Pionus parrots in captivity. These efforts were crucial in maintaining healthy populations and reducing the reliance on wild-caught birds, which contributed to the conservation of their natural habitats.

Modern Aviculture and Conservation

Today, Pionus parrots are well-established in aviculture worldwide. Breeding programs and avian enthusiasts have succeeded in maintaining healthy captive populations, and Pionus parrots are now commonly available in the pet trade. They are especially popular in North America and Europe, where their gentle nature and engaging personalities make them sought-after pets.

Despite their success in captivity, conservation efforts remain important to protect wild populations. Habitat destruction and illegal trapping pose significant threats to many parrot species, including Pionus. Conservation organizations work to preserve the natural habitats of these birds and promote sustainable practices within local communities.

Pionus Parrots in Research and Education

Pionus parrots have also played a role in scientific research and education. Their relatively calm temperament makes them suitable subjects for studies on avian behavior, cognition, and communication. Research on Pionus parrots has contributed to a better understanding of parrot social structures, vocalizations, and problem-solving abilities.

In educational settings, Pionus parrots are often used in programs to teach people about avian biology, conservation, and responsible pet ownership. Their manageable size and gentle nature make them ideal ambassadors for promoting awareness about parrot care and conservation efforts.

The history and background of Pionus parrots reflect their journey from the wilds of Central and South America to becoming cherished companions in households around the world. Their adaptability, unique physical characteristics, and engaging personalities have endeared them to aviculturists and pet owners alike. Understanding the historical context of these parrots enhances our appreciation for their presence in both the wild and our lives, highlighting the importance of ongoing conservation and responsible aviculture practices.

1.3 Why Choose a Pionus Parrot as a Pet?

Choosing a pet bird involves considering various factors such as temperament, care requirements, lifespan, and the ability to bond with humans. Pionus parrots, with their unique characteristics and relatively manageable care needs, stand out as excellent companions for both novice and experienced bird owners. Here are the key reasons why choosing a Pionus parrot as a pet can be a rewarding experience.

Temperament and Personality

One of the most appealing aspects of Pionus parrots is their generally calm and gentle temperament. Unlike some parrot species that can be highly demanding and noisy, Pionus parrots are known for their quieter demeanor. They tend to be less prone to screaming and can adapt well to a home environment without causing significant noise disturbances, making them suitable for apartment living.

Pionus parrots are also known for their affectionate and sociable nature. While they may not be as overtly cuddly as some other parrots, they form strong bonds with their owners and enjoy spending time with them. They appreciate interaction and can become quite attached to their human companions, often displaying affectionate behaviors such as head bobbing, gentle nipping, and mimicking sounds.

Intelligence and Trainability

Pionus parrots are intelligent birds capable of learning a variety of tricks and behaviors. Their cognitive abilities make them responsive to training, which can include learning to step up on command, performing simple tricks, and even mimicking speech and sounds. While they may not be as prolific talkers as African Greys or Amazon parrots, Pionus parrots can learn to say a few words and phrases, adding to their charm.

Training a Pionus parrot can be a rewarding experience for both the bird and the owner. Positive reinforcement techniques, such as using treats and praise, work well with these parrots. Training sessions also provide mental stimulation, helping to prevent boredom and related behavioral issues.

Manageable Size and Care Requirements

Pionus parrots are medium-sized birds, typically measuring between 10 to 12 inches in length. Their manageable size makes them easier to house and care for compared to larger parrot species. They require a spacious cage that allows for movement and play, but their moderate size means they do not need the extremely large enclosures required by some other parrots.

In terms of diet, Pionus parrots thrive on a balanced diet of high-quality pellets, fresh fruits, and vegetables. Their dietary needs are relatively straightforward, and with proper care, they can maintain good health. Regular veterinary check-ups are essential to monitor their health and catch any potential issues early.

Long Lifespan and Commitment

Pionus parrots have a relatively long lifespan, often living between 25 to 40 years with proper care. This longevity means that choosing a Pionus parrot as a pet is a long-term commitment. Potential owners should be prepared for the responsibility of caring for their bird throughout its life, which includes providing consistent attention, a proper diet, and regular health care.

The long lifespan of Pionus parrots can be a significant advantage for those looking for a long-term companion. They become integral members of the family, and their presence can bring joy and companionship for many years.

Low Allergen Risk

One practical advantage of Pionus parrots is that they tend to produce less dander compared to some other parrot species. This makes them a more suitable option for individuals who are sensitive to allergens. While no bird is completely hypoallergenic, the lower dander production in Pionus parrots can result in fewer allergy-related issues for their owners.

Compatibility with Families and Other Pets

Pionus parrots are generally good with families, including children, provided the interactions are supervised and respectful. Their gentle nature makes them less likely to exhibit aggressive behaviors, and they can become affectionate companions for family members of all ages.

When it comes to other pets, Pionus parrots can coexist peacefully with other birds and even some non-avian pets, provided proper introductions are made, and their interactions are monitored. It's essential to ensure that the parrot's safety and well-being are prioritized in a multi-pet household.

Enrichment and Engagement

Keeping a Pionus parrot mentally stimulated is crucial for their well-being. These parrots enjoy a variety of toys, puzzles, and activities that challenge their intelligence and curiosity. Providing a range of enrichment options, such as foraging toys, climbing structures, and interactive play, helps keep them engaged and happy.

Owners who invest time in creating an enriching environment for their Pionus parrot will find that these birds are highly responsive and eager to engage in new activities. This level of interaction fosters a strong bond between the parrot and the owner, enhancing the overall pet ownership experience.

Choosing a Pionus parrot as a pet offers numerous benefits, from their gentle temperament and manageable size to their intelligence and long lifespan. These parrots are suitable for a wide range of households, including those living in apartments and families with children. Their ability to form strong bonds with their owners, combined with their relatively low noise levels and straightforward care requirements, makes them an attractive option for bird enthusiasts.

By understanding the unique qualities of Pionus parrots and providing them with the appropriate care, attention, and enrichment, owners can enjoy a fulfilling and lasting relationship with these delightful and engaging birds.

CHAPTER TWO

Pionus Parrot Species Overview

2.1 Common Species of Pionus Parrots

Pionus parrots are a captivating group of medium-sized parrots known for their robust bodies, vibrant plumage, and calm demeanor. Eight recognized species belong to the genus **Pionus**, each with distinct characteristics that make them unique. Here is an extensive overview of the common species of Pionus parrots, highlighting their physical traits, natural habitats, behaviors, and suitability as pets.

1. Blue-headed Pionus (Pionus menstruus)

Fig 2: Blue-headed Pionus

Physical Characteristics:

i. Size: Approximately 11 inches (28 cm) in length.

ii. Weight: Around 250 to 280 grams.

iii. Plumage: Predominantly green body with a striking blue head and neck. The under-tail coverts are red, and there is a slight pinkish hue on the throat.

Natural Habitat:

i. Found in a wide range from Central America (southern Mexico) through the Amazon Basin in South America.

ii. Inhabit tropical and subtropical forests, including lowland rainforests, foothill forests, and wooded areas.

Behavior:

i. Known for their gentle and relatively quiet nature.

ii. Sociable and curious, they enjoy interacting with their owners and exploring their environment.

iii. Capable of mimicking sounds and words, though not as prolific as some other parrot species.

Suitability as Pets:

i. Ideal for families and individuals due to their manageable size and calm demeanor.

ii. Require a spacious cage, a balanced diet of pellets, fruits, and vegetables, and regular mental stimulation through toys and interaction.

2. Maximilian's Pionus (Pionus maximiliani)

Physical Characteristics:

i. Size: About 11 inches (28 cm) in length.

ii. Weight: Ranges from 240 to 290 grams.

iii. Plumage: Green body with a bluish tinge on the head and neck. The under-tail coverts are red, and there is a dusky blue coloration on the chest.

Fig 3: Maximilian's Pionus

Natural Habitat:

i. Native to Brazil, Bolivia, Paraguay, and northern Argentina.

ii. Prefers forested areas, including rainforests, woodlands, and savannas.

Behavior:

i. Often described as even-tempered and easygoing.

ii. Less likely to scream compared to other parrot species, making them suitable for quieter households.

iii. Enjoys socializing with humans and can develop strong bonds with their owners.

Suitability as Pets:

i. Good choice for first-time parrot owners due to their stable temperament.

ii. Needs a balanced diet, regular veterinary check-ups, and plenty of social interaction and mental stimulation.

3. White-crowned Pionus (Pionus senilis)

Fig 4: White-crowned Pionus

Physical Characteristics:

i. Size: Approximately 10 inches (25 cm) in length.

ii. Weight: Around 200 to 240 grams.

iii. Plumage: Green body with a distinctive white crown. The throat and upper breast are blue, and the under-tail coverts are red.

Natural Habitat:

i. Found in Central America, from southern Mexico to western Panama.

ii. Inhabit lowland and montane forests, often at higher elevations than other Pionus species.

Behavior:

i. Known for their playful and inquisitive nature.

ii. Can be more vocal than other Pionus species, but still relatively quiet compared to many parrots.

iii. Enjoys exploring and playing with a variety of toys.

Suitability as Pets:

i. Suitable for families and individuals who can provide ample interaction and mental enrichment.

ii. Requires a varied diet, including high-quality pellets, fresh fruits, and vegetables, along with a spacious and enriching environment.

4. Dusky Pionus (Pionus fuscus)

Physical Characteristics:

i. Size: About 10 to 11 inches (25 to 28 cm) in length.

ii. Weight: Approximately 200 to 240 grams.

iii. Plumage: Dark, dusky blue coloration with a greenish tinge on the back and wings. The under-tail coverts are red, and the throat may have a pinkish hue.

Fig 5: Dusky Pionus

Natural Habitat:

i. Found in the northern regions of South America, including Venezuela, Guyana, Suriname, and northern Brazil.

ii. Inhabit humid lowland forests and forest edges.

Behavior:

i. Known for their relatively quiet and calm nature.

ii. Can be shy initially but become affectionate and playful with consistent interaction.

iii. Enjoys foraging and exploring their environment.

Suitability as Pets:

i. Ideal for those seeking a quieter parrot with a gentle temperament.

ii. Needs a well-balanced diet, regular social interaction, and a variety of toys to keep them mentally stimulated.

5. Bronze-winged Pionus (Pionus chalcopterus)

Physical Characteristics:

i. Size: Approximately 11 inches (28 cm) in length.

ii. Weight: Around 240 to 290 grams.

iii. Plumage: Dark green body with bronze-colored wings. The head and neck are bluish-purple, and the under-tail coverts are red.

Fig 6: Bronze-winged Pionus

Natural Habitat:

i. Native to the Andean regions of South America, including Colombia, Ecuador, and Peru.

ii. Inhabit humid montane forests and cloud forests, often at higher elevations.

Behavior:

i. Known for their friendly and affectionate nature.

ii. Relatively quiet and can develop a strong bond with their owners.

iii. Enjoys climbing and playing with a variety of toys.

Suitability as Pets:

i. Suitable for families and individuals who can provide regular social interaction and mental stimulation.

ii. Requires a diet rich in fruits, vegetables, and high-quality pellets, along with a spacious and enriching environment.

6. Coral-billed Pionus (Pionus sordidus)

Fig 7: Coral-billed Pionus

Physical Characteristics:

i. Size: About 11 inches (28 cm) in length.

ii. Weight: Approximately 200 to 250 grams.

iii. Plumage: Green body with a bronze tint on the upper parts. The head and neck are dull purple, and the under-tail coverts are red. The bill is coral-colored.

Natural Habitat:

i. Found in northern South America, including Colombia, Venezuela, and Trinidad.

ii. Inhabit lowland rainforests and forest edges.

Behavior:

i. Known for their calm and gentle disposition.

ii. Less vocal compared to some other parrot species, making them suitable for quieter households.

iii. Enjoys interacting with their owners and exploring their environment.

Suitability as Pets:

i. Good choice for individuals and families seeking a quieter, more relaxed parrot.

ii. Needs a balanced diet, regular veterinary care, and plenty of mental and physical stimulation.

7. Plum-crowned Pionus (Pionus tumultuosus)

Physical Characteristics:

i. Size: Approximately 11 inches (28 cm) in length.

ii. Weight: Around 200 to 240 grams.

iii. Plumage: Green body with a distinctive plum-colored crown and nape. The under-tail coverts are red.

Fig 8: Plum-crowned Pionus

Natural Habitat:

i. Found in the Andean regions of South America, including Peru and Bolivia.

ii. Inhabit montane forests and cloud forests at high elevations.

Behavior:

i. Known for their quiet and gentle nature.

ii. Can be shy initially but becomes more confident with consistent interaction.

iii. Enjoys foraging and exploring their environment.

Suitability as Pets:

i. Suitable for individuals and families who can provide a quiet and stable environment.

ii. Requires a diet rich in fruits, vegetables, and high-quality pellets, along with a variety of toys for mental stimulation.

8. Scaly-headed Pionus (Pionus maximiliani melanoblepharus)

Fig 9: Scaly-headed Pionus

Physical Characteristics:

i. Size: About 11 inches (28 cm) in length.

ii. Weight: Approximately 240 to 290 grams.

iii. Plumage: Green body with a scaly pattern on the head and neck. The under-tail coverts are red, and there is a bluish tinge on the wings.

Natural Habitat:

i. Found in Brazil, Paraguay, and northern Argentina.

ii. Inhabit a variety of forested areas, including rainforests, woodlands, and savannas.

Behavior:

i. Known for their even-tempered and friendly nature.

ii. Less likely to scream compared to other parrot species, making them suitable for quieter households.

iii. Enjoys socializing with humans and playing with a variety of toys.

Suitability as Pets:

i. Good choice for first-time parrot owners due to their stable temperament.

ii. Needs a balanced diet, regular veterinary check-ups, and plenty of social interaction and mental stimulation.

Each species of Pionus parrot has its unique characteristics and charm, making them appealing to a wide range of bird enthusiasts. Whether you are looking for a quiet and gentle companion or a playful and affectionate pet, there is likely a Pionus parrot species that will suit your preferences and lifestyle. Understanding the distinct traits and needs of these parrots is essential for providing them with a happy and healthy life as a cherished member of your household.

2.2 Physical Characteristics and Color Variations

Pionus parrots are known for their robust build, vibrant plumage, and distinctive physical traits. While they share some common characteristics, each species within the genus **Pionus** exhibits unique features and color variations that set them apart. Understanding these differences can help potential owners identify and appreciate the beauty and diversity of Pionus parrots.

General Physical Characteristics

1. Size and Build:

Size: Pionus parrots are medium-sized birds, typically ranging from 10 to 12 inches (25 to 30 cm) in length.

Weight: They generally weigh between 200 to 300 grams, with some variation depending on the species.

Build: These parrots have a robust, stocky build with a broad chest and short, square tails. Their bodies are well-proportioned, and they have strong legs and feet adapted for climbing and perching.

2. Head and Beak:

Head: Pionus parrots have relatively large heads in proportion to their bodies. Their heads are often adorned with distinctive color patterns that vary by species.

Beak: They possess a strong, curved beak that is well-suited for cracking nuts and seeds. The beak color can vary, often complementing the bird's plumage.

3. Eyes and Eye Ring:

Eyes: The eyes of Pionus parrots are expressive and can range in color from dark brown to reddish-brown.

Eye Ring: One of the most distinctive features of Pionus parrots is the bare, fleshy eye ring that surrounds their eyes. The color of the eye ring can differ among species, adding to their unique appearance.

4. Feet and Legs:

Feet: Pionus parrots have zygodactyl feet, meaning they have two toes pointing forward and two toes pointing backward. This foot structure aids in their climbing and perching abilities.

Legs: Their legs are sturdy and strong, allowing them to navigate their environment with ease.

Species-Specific Color Variations

1. Blue-headed Pionus (Pionus menstruus):

Plumage: The Blue-headed Pionus is renowned for its striking blue head and neck. The body is predominantly green, with a red patch on the under-tail coverts. The throat may exhibit a pinkish hue.

Eye Ring: The eye ring is white, contrasting sharply with the blue head.

2. Maximilian's Pionus (Pionus maximiliani):

Plumage: This species has a green body with bluish accents on the head, neck, and wings. The under-tail coverts are red, and there is often a dusky blue coloration on the chest.

Eye Ring: The eye ring is grey, blending subtly with the surrounding plumage.

3. White-crowned Pionus (Pionus senilis):

Plumage: The White-crowned Pionus features a green body with a distinctive white crown on the head. The throat and upper breast are blue, and the under-tail coverts are red.

Eye Ring: The eye ring is greyish-white, complementing the white crown.

4. Dusky Pionus (Pionus fuscus):

Plumage: The Dusky Pionus has a dark, dusky blue body with a greenish tinge on the back and wings. The under-tail coverts are red, and the throat may have a pinkish hue.

Eye Ring: The eye ring is dark grey, blending with the dusky plumage.

5. Bronze-winged Pionus (Pionus chalcopterus):

Plumage: This species boasts a dark green body with bronze-colored wings. The head and neck are bluish-purple, and the under-tail coverts are red.

Eye Ring: The eye ring is pink, providing a striking contrast to the dark plumage.

6. Coral-billed Pionus (Pionus sordidus):

Plumage: The Coral-billed Pionus has a green body with a bronze tint on the upper parts. The head and neck are dull purple, and the under-tail coverts are red. The bill is coral-colored.

Eye Ring: The eye ring is pale pink, matching the coral bill.

7. Plum-crowned Pionus (Pionus tumultuosus):

Plumage: The Plum-crowned Pionus features a green body with a distinctive plum-colored crown and nape. The under-tail coverts are red.

Eye Ring: The eye ring is pale pink, harmonizing with the plum-colored crown.

8. Scaly-headed Pionus (Pionus maximiliani melanoblepharus):

Plumage: This subspecies of Maximilian's Pionus has a green body with a scaly pattern on the head and neck. The under-tail coverts are red, and there is a bluish tinge on the wings.

Eye Ring: The eye ring is grey, blending subtly with the scaly pattern on the head.

Color Mutations and Variations

In addition to the natural color variations found in wild Pionus parrots, captive breeding has produced several color mutations. These mutations are the result of selective breeding and can enhance or alter the natural colors of the parrots. Some of the common color mutations include:

1. Blue Mutation:

This mutation enhances the blue pigmentation in the parrot's plumage, resulting in a more vibrant and extensive blue coloration, often replacing the green areas.

2. Albino Mutation:

Albino Pionus parrots lack melanin, resulting in a white or pale plumage with red or pink eyes. This mutation is rare and can affect the bird's overall health and vision.

3. Lutino Mutation:

Lutino Pionus parrots have a bright yellow or golden plumage due to the absence of certain pigments. They also have red or pink eyes, similar to albino mutations.

4. Pied Mutation:

Pied Pionus parrots exhibit irregular patches of different colors, often a mix of white, yellow, and the bird's natural colors. This mutation creates a unique and striking appearance.

Sexual Dimorphism

Pionus parrots do not exhibit strong sexual dimorphism, meaning males and females generally look alike. However, slight differences in size and coloration may be observed in some species, but these are usually subtle and not easily noticeable without close inspection or genetic testing.

Juvenile and Adult Plumage

Juvenile Pionus parrots often have duller plumage compared to adults. As they mature, their colors become more vibrant and distinctive. The transition from juvenile to adult plumage can take several months to a few years, depending on the species and individual bird.

The physical characteristics and color variations of Pionus parrots make them a visually stunning and diverse group of birds. Their robust build, expressive eyes, and vibrant plumage contribute to their appeal as pets. Each species within the genus **Pionus** has unique features that set them apart, providing bird enthusiasts with a range of options to choose from. Understanding these characteristics helps in appreciating the beauty and individuality of each Pionus parrot, enhancing the experience of keeping them as cherished companions.

2.3 Understanding Pionus Parrot Behavior

Pionus parrots are known for their gentle temperament, intelligence, and sociable nature, making them delightful companions for bird enthusiasts. Understanding their behavior is essential for providing appropriate care, building a strong bond, and ensuring their well-being in a home environment. Here's an extensive overview of Pionus parrot behavior, including their social interactions, communication methods, natural instincts, and common behaviors exhibited in captivity.

Social Interactions

1. Bonding with Humans:

i. Pionus parrots are naturally social birds that can form strong bonds with their owners. They enjoy interacting with humans and thrive on companionship.

ii. They are known for their gentle and affectionate nature, often displaying behaviors such as head bobbing, preening, and gentle nipping as signs of affection.

iii. Building trust through positive reinforcement and spending quality time together helps strengthen the bond between a Pionus parrot and its owner.

2. Interaction with Other Pets:

i. Pionus parrots can coexist peacefully with other birds and some non-avian pets, provided proper introductions and supervision are maintained.

ii. They may display curiosity towards other pets and can develop companionship bonds with them, depending on individual personalities and socialization experiences.

3. Flock Mentality:

i. In the wild, Pionus parrots are social flock birds that rely on each other for companionship, safety, and foraging.

ii. In captivity, they often view their human family as part of their flock and seek social interaction and inclusion in daily activities.

Communication Methods

1. Vocalizations:

i. Pionus parrots are relatively quiet compared to some other parrot species, making them suitable for apartment living or quieter households.

ii. Their vocal repertoire includes soft chirps, whistles, and occasional squawks. They may also mimic environmental sounds or words, though they are not as prolific talkers as some larger parrot species.

2. Body Language:

i. Body language plays a crucial role in Pionus parrot communication. Common gestures include head bobbing, wing fluttering, and tail fanning.

ii. Preening is a social behavior that reinforces bonding among flock members and is also seen in pet Pionus parrots as a sign of contentment and well-being.

3. Visual Signals:

i. Pionus parrots use visual cues such as eye pinning (rapid dilation and contraction of the pupils), body posture, and facial expressions to convey their mood and intentions.

ii. They may raise their crest feathers when excited or alert and lower them when relaxed or content.

Natural Instincts and Behaviors

1. Foraging Behavior:

i. Pionus parrots are natural foragers, spending time in the wild searching for food sources such as fruits, seeds, nuts, and vegetation.

ii. In captivity, replicating this natural behavior through foraging toys and puzzles helps stimulate their cognitive abilities and provides enrichment.

2. Bathing and Grooming:

i. Pionus parrots enjoy bathing and should be provided with opportunities to bathe regularly. This can be accomplished through misting with water or providing a shallow dish for them to splash in.

ii. Grooming, including preening their feathers, is essential for maintaining their plumage and health. Pionus parrots often preen themselves and their bonded companions as a social activity.

3. Play and Enrichment:

i. Play is an integral part of a Pionus parrot's daily routine. They enjoy playing with toys that encourage physical activity, mental stimulation, and problem-solving.

ii. Enrichment activities such as exploring new toys, foraging for treats, and participating in training sessions help prevent boredom and promote a healthy, active lifestyle.

Common Behaviors in Captivity

1. Territoriality:

Pionus parrots may exhibit territorial behavior, particularly around their cage or preferred perching areas. This behavior is natural and can be managed through appropriate cage placement and environmental enrichment.

2. Vocalizations:

While generally quieter than many other parrot species, Pionus parrots may vocalize to express excitement, seek attention, or communicate their needs. Understanding their vocal cues and responding appropriately helps strengthen the bond between the bird and its owner.

3. Affectionate Gestures:

Pionus parrots demonstrate affection through gentle behaviors such as cuddling, preening, and vocalizing softly. They may also enjoy physical contact, such as being gently scratched on the head or neck, as a form of bonding with their human companions.

Behavioral Challenges and Solutions

1. Boredom and Stereotypic Behaviors:

Boredom can lead to stereotypic behaviors such as feather plucking or excessive vocalization. Providing a stimulating environment with varied toys, social interaction, and regular out-of-cage time can help prevent boredom and associated behavioral issues.

2. Training and Positive Reinforcement:

Training Pionus parrots using positive reinforcement techniques, such as offering treats and praise, can help shape desirable behaviors and strengthen the bond between bird and owner. Consistent and patient training sessions promote mental stimulation and encourage learning.

Understanding Pionus parrot behavior is key to providing them with a nurturing and enriching environment in captivity. Their gentle temperament, social nature, and intelligence make them rewarding companions for bird enthusiasts. By recognizing their communication methods, natural instincts, and common behaviors, owners can foster a strong bond with their Pionus parrot while promoting their physical and mental health. Meeting their social, cognitive, and physical needs ensures that these delightful birds thrive and flourish as cherished members of the family.

CHAPTER THREE

Getting Started: Preparing for Your Pionus Parrot

3.1 Legal Considerations and Regulations

Owning and caring for a Pionus parrot involves understanding and adhering to various legal considerations and regulations, which vary depending on your location. These guidelines are essential to ensure the well-being of the birds and compliance with local laws. Here's an extensive overview of legal considerations and regulations related to Pionus parrots:

Legal Status and Protection

1. Wildlife Protection Laws:

Pionus parrots, like all wild birds, are protected under various wildlife protection laws in many countries. These laws regulate the capture, trade, import, export, and ownership of wild-caught and captive-bred parrots to prevent exploitation and ensure conservation.

2. CITES Listing:

The Convention on International Trade in Endangered Species of Wild Fauna and Flora (CITES) lists some species of Pionus parrots under Appendix II. Species listed under CITES Appendix II require permits for international trade to ensure that their capture and trade do not threaten their survival in the wild.

3. National and Regional Regulations:

Countries and regions may have specific regulations governing the ownership, breeding, sale, and transport of Pionus parrots. These regulations often include requirements for permits, licenses, and health certifications for owning and trading parrots.

Import and Export Regulations

1. International Trade Regulations:

Import and export of Pionus parrots across international borders are subject to regulations set by CITES and national wildlife authorities. Proper documentation, including CITES permits or equivalent, is required to legally transport Pionus parrots between countries.

2. Quarantine Requirements:

Many countries have quarantine regulations for imported birds to prevent the spread of diseases. Pionus parrots may need to undergo quarantine and health screenings upon arrival to ensure they are free from diseases that could affect native wildlife and domestic birds.

Ownership and Captive Breeding

1. Captive Breeding Programs:

Encouraging captive breeding of Pionus parrots helps reduce the demand for wild-caught birds and supports conservation efforts. Some countries provide incentives or support for captive breeding programs through grants, permits, or tax incentives.

2. Ownership Permits:

Depending on your location, ownership of Pionus parrots may require permits or licenses from wildlife authorities. These permits may involve criteria such as ensuring proper housing, care, and conditions for the birds.

Welfare and Ethical Considerations

1. Responsible Ownership:

Responsible ownership of Pionus parrots includes providing appropriate housing, nutrition, veterinary care, and enrichment. Owners should be knowledgeable about the species' needs and behaviors to ensure their physical and psychological well-being.

2. Ethical Considerations:

Ethical considerations in owning Pionus parrots involve respecting their natural behaviors, social needs, and ensuring they are not subjected to stress or mistreatment. Avoiding practices that harm wild populations, such as supporting illegal wildlife trade or capturing birds from the wild, is crucial for their conservation.

Local Regulations and Resources

1. Wildlife Authorities:

Contact local wildlife authorities or government agencies responsible for wildlife management to inquire about specific regulations and requirements for owning Pionus parrots. These authorities can provide information on permits, licensing, and legal responsibilities associated with owning and caring for these birds.

2. Conservation Organizations:

Conservation organizations and bird clubs often provide resources, education, and guidelines for responsible parrot ownership. They may also offer support for conservation initiatives and promote sustainable practices in the pet trade industry.

Navigating legal considerations and regulations is essential for anyone interested in owning or caring for Pionus parrots. By understanding and complying with wildlife protection laws, import/export regulations, ownership permits, and ethical considerations, owners can ensure the welfare of their birds and contribute to conservation efforts. Staying informed about local laws and seeking guidance from wildlife authorities and conservation organizations helps foster responsible stewardship of these beautiful and intelligent birds in captivity.

3.2 Choosing the Right Pionus Parrot for You

Choosing a Pionus parrot as a pet is a significant decision that requires careful consideration of various factors. Each species within the Pionus genus has unique characteristics, temperaments, and care requirements. Understanding these aspects will help you select the right Pionus parrot that aligns with your lifestyle, preferences, and ability to provide proper care.

Here's an extensive guide to choosing the right Pionus parrot for you:

Understanding Pionus Parrot Species

1. Species Variability:

The genus Pionus includes several species, each with distinct physical traits and colorations. Common species include the Blue-headed Pionus, Maximilian's Pionus, White-crowned Pionus, Dusky Pionus, Bronze-winged Pionus, Coral-billed Pionus, Plum-crowned Pionus, and Scaly-headed Pionus. Researching each species' characteristics, including size, coloration, vocalizations, and behavior, will help you identify which Pionus parrot best suits your preferences.

2. Temperament and Personality:

i. Pionus parrots are generally known for their gentle and calm demeanor compared to larger parrot species.

ii. However, individual birds may exhibit variations in temperament. Some may be more outgoing and sociable, while others may be quieter or more reserved.

iii. Spending time interacting with different Pionus parrots can help you gauge their personality and compatibility with your lifestyle.

Considerations for Potential Owners

1. Experience Level:

i. Pionus parrots are suitable for both novice and experienced bird owners.

ii. Novice owners may find Pionus parrots appealing due to their manageable size, gentle nature, and lower noise levels compared to some other parrot species.

iii. Experienced owners can appreciate the unique traits and behaviors of Pionus parrots, as well as their potential for forming strong bonds with their human companions.

2. Living Arrangements:

i. Consider your living situation, including the size of your home, noise tolerance, and proximity to neighbors, when choosing a Pionus parrot.

ii. Pionus parrots are quieter than many other parrot species but still require adequate space and environmental enrichment.

iii. Ensure you have a suitable cage or aviary that provides enough room for the bird to move around comfortably and engage in natural behaviors.

3. Time Commitment:

i. Pionus parrots are social birds that thrive on interaction with their human caregivers.

ii. They require daily mental stimulation, socialization, and exercise to maintain their well-being.

iii. Consider your daily schedule and ability to dedicate time to interacting with and caring for your Pionus parrot before making a commitment.

Health and Care Requirements

1. Veterinary Care:

Regular veterinary check-ups are essential to monitor the health of your Pionus parrot and detect any potential health issues early. Find an avian veterinarian experienced with Pionus parrots who can provide preventive care, vaccinations, and treatment if needed.

2. Diet and Nutrition:

Pionus parrots require a balanced diet consisting of high-quality pellets, fresh fruits, vegetables, and occasional treats such as nuts and seeds. Providing a variety of foods ensures they receive essential nutrients and prevents dietary deficiencies.

3. Enrichment and Mental Stimulation:

Enrichment activities are crucial for the mental and physical well-being of Pionus parrots. Offer a variety of toys, puzzles, foraging opportunities, and social interaction to prevent boredom and encourage natural behaviors.

Interaction and Bonding

1. Socialization Needs:

i. Pionus parrots enjoy interacting with their human caregivers and thrive on companionship.

ii. Spend time daily talking to, playing with, and training your Pionus parrot to build trust and strengthen your bond.

2. Training and Behavior:

i. Positive reinforcement training methods can help shape desirable behaviors and teach basic commands.

ii. Understand and respect your Pionus parrot's natural behaviors, such as preening, vocalizations, and body language, to facilitate effective communication.

Considerations for Multiple Parrots

1. Compatibility:

i. If considering multiple Pionus parrots or other bird species, ensure they are compatible in terms of temperament and social dynamics.

ii. Provide separate housing and supervised interaction until you are confident they can coexist peacefully.

2. Potential Challenges:

i. Be prepared for potential challenges, such as introducing new birds, managing territorial behavior, and preventing aggression.

ii. Seek guidance from experienced bird owners or avian behaviorists if needed to address behavioral issues.

Choosing the right Pionus parrot involves thorough research, consideration of your lifestyle and experience level, and understanding the specific needs and characteristics of each species. By evaluating factors such as temperament, health care requirements, living arrangements, and interaction preferences, you can make an informed decision that ensures a rewarding and fulfilling relationship with your Pionus parrot. Responsible ownership, proper care, and dedication to meeting their needs will contribute to a long and happy life for your feathered companion.

3.3 Setting Up the Ideal Habitat and Cage for Pionus Parrots

Creating an ideal habitat and providing a suitable cage is crucial for the health, well-being, and happiness of Pionus parrots. These birds thrive in environments that mimic their natural habitat while offering safety, comfort, and opportunities for mental stimulation. Here's an extensive guide on setting up the ideal habitat and cage for your Pionus parrot:

Understanding Pionus Parrot Habitat Needs

1. Space Requirements:

i. Pionus parrots are medium-sized birds that require ample space to move around freely.

ii. The minimum recommended cage size for a single Pionus parrot should be at least 24 inches (60 cm) wide, 24 inches (60 cm) deep, and 36 inches (90 cm) high.

iii. Larger cages or aviaries are preferable, as they provide more room for exercise, wing stretching, and natural behaviors.

2. Cage Bar Spacing:

i. Choose a cage with horizontal bars spaced no more than 3/4 inch (1.9 cm) apart to prevent injury or escape.

ii. Horizontal bars allow the parrot to climb and exercise, which is essential for their physical and mental health.

3. Cage Location:

i. Place the cage in a quiet area of your home away from drafts, direct sunlight, and household hazards.

ii. Ensure the cage is secure and stable, away from areas with heavy foot traffic or loud noises that may stress the bird.

Cage Features and Accessories

1. Perches:

i. Provide a variety of perch sizes and textures to encourage natural foot exercise and prevent foot problems.

ii. Natural wood perches of different diameters (1/2 to 1 1/2 inches or 1.3 to 3.8 cm) are ideal, as they mimic branches found in the wild.

2. Feeding Dishes and Water Containers:

i. Use stainless steel or ceramic dishes for food and water to prevent chewing and contamination.

ii. Place dishes at a comfortable height for easy access, ensuring they are securely attached to prevent spills.

3. Toys and Enrichment:

i. Offer a selection of toys that stimulate the bird's mind and encourage physical activity.

ii. Toys should include chewable items, puzzles, swings, and foraging toys to prevent boredom and promote mental stimulation.

iii. Rotate toys regularly to maintain interest and provide new challenges.

4. Cage Substrate:

i. Line the bottom of the cage with safe substrate, such as paper or bird-safe bedding, to absorb droppings.

ii. Avoid using substrates that may be harmful if ingested, such as cedar or pine shavings.

5. Hideouts and Nesting Areas:

i. Provide hideouts or nest boxes where the bird can retreat for privacy and security.

ii. Nest boxes are especially important for breeding pairs or birds that prefer enclosed spaces for resting.

Environmental Enrichment

1. Natural Branches and Greens:

i. Incorporate natural branches from non-toxic trees (e.g., apple, willow) to simulate perching in the wild.

ii. Fresh, bird-safe leafy greens can be offered as occasional treats and provide enrichment.

2. Environmental Variation:

i. Create a dynamic environment by varying the placement of perches, toys, and feeding stations within the cage.

ii. Offer different textures, colors, and materials to stimulate the bird's senses and encourage exploration.

3. Out-of-Cage Time:

i. Allow supervised out-of-cage time in a safe, bird-proofed area to promote exercise, social interaction, and mental stimulation.

ii. Ensure the space is free from hazards such as toxic plants, electrical cords, and small objects that could be ingested.

Cleaning and Maintenance

1. Regular Cleaning Routine:

i. Establish a regular cleaning schedule to maintain hygiene and prevent the buildup of waste and bacteria.

ii. Clean food and water dishes daily, replace substrate as needed, and thoroughly clean the cage and accessories weekly.

2. Cage Safety Checks:

i. Inspect the cage regularly for any signs of wear, damage, or potential hazards.

ii. Ensure all locks, latches, and perches are secure to prevent escapes or injuries.

Temperature and Humidity

1. Optimal Temperature Range:

i. Pionus parrots are adaptable to a range of temperatures but prefer stable conditions between 65-80°F (18-27°C).

ii. Avoid placing the cage near drafts or heating/cooling vents that may cause temperature fluctuations.

2. Humidity Levels:

i. Maintain moderate humidity levels between 40-70% to support respiratory health and prevent dryness.

ii. Use a room humidifier or mist the bird occasionally if the air is too dry, especially during winter months.

Creating an ideal habitat and providing a well-equipped cage is essential for the overall health, happiness, and enrichment of Pionus parrots. By understanding their natural behaviors, space requirements, and environmental needs, you can design a safe and stimulating environment that promotes physical activity, mental well-being, and social interaction. Regular maintenance, enrichment activities, and monitoring of environmental conditions will ensure that your Pionus parrot thrives and enjoys a fulfilling life in captivity. Investing time and effort into setting up the ideal habitat will contribute to a strong bond and a rewarding companionship with your feathered friend.

CHAPTER FOUR

Pionus Parrot Diet and Nutrition

4.1 Essential Nutritional Needs of Pionus Parrots

Providing a balanced and nutritious diet is crucial for the health, longevity, and well-being of Pionus parrots. These birds have specific dietary requirements that must be met to support their growth, immune function, and overall vitality. Understanding their nutritional needs involves knowledge of their natural diet, essential nutrients, potential dietary deficiencies, and recommended feeding practices. Here's an extensive guide to the essential nutritional needs of Pionus parrots:

Natural Diet in the Wild

1. Omnivorous Diet:

i. Pionus parrots in the wild are omnivorous, consuming a varied diet that includes fruits, seeds, nuts, berries, flowers, buds, and occasionally insects.

ii. Their natural foraging behavior involves searching for food sources in trees and on the ground, which stimulates physical activity and mental engagement.

2. Seed Preferences:

i. Pionus parrots have a preference for seeds and nuts, especially during certain seasons when these food sources are abundant.

ii. While seeds are enjoyed, they should not constitute the majority of their diet in captivity due to potential nutritional imbalances.

Essential Nutrients

1. Balanced Diet Components:

i. A balanced diet for Pionus parrots should include a variety of foods to ensure they receive essential nutrients.

ii. Key components include high-quality pellets, fresh fruits, vegetables, leafy greens, grains, nuts, and occasional protein sources such as cooked eggs or lean meats (e.g., chicken or turkey).

2. Macronutrients:

i. Protein: Essential for growth, tissue repair, and immune function. Sources include pellets, legumes, and small amounts of lean animal protein.

ii. Carbohydrates: Provide energy and should come from whole grains, vegetables, and fruits.

iii. Fats: Important for energy, insulation, and maintaining healthy skin and feathers. Offer healthy fats from nuts, seeds, and occasional avocados.

3. Vitamins and Minerals:

i. Vitamin A: Crucial for vision, skin health, and immune function. Found in orange and dark green vegetables, carrots, and sweet potatoes.

ii. Vitamin D: Supports calcium absorption and bone health. Natural sunlight exposure or vitamin D3 supplements may be necessary.

iii. Calcium: Essential for strong bones, eggshell formation (for breeding females), and muscle function. Offer calcium-rich foods like dark leafy greens, broccoli, and fortified pellets.

iv. Iron: Important for oxygen transport in the blood. Green vegetables, legumes, and fortified cereals provide iron.

v. Iodine: Necessary for thyroid function and metabolism. Seafood, iodized salt (in small amounts), and seaweed are good sources.

Common Nutritional Deficiencies

1. Vitamin A Deficiency:

i. Insufficient intake of vitamin A can lead to respiratory infections, skin and feather problems, and poor vision.

ii. Provide foods rich in beta-carotene (converted to vitamin A), such as sweet potatoes, carrots, and dark leafy greens.

2. Calcium Deficiency:

i. Inadequate calcium levels can result in brittle bones, egg-binding (in females), and muscle weakness.

ii. Offer calcium supplements or calcium-rich foods and monitor calcium-to-phosphorus ratio in the diet.

3. Protein Deficiency:

i. Insufficient protein intake can lead to poor growth, feather abnormalities, and weakened immune function.

ii. Ensure protein sources are varied and include pellets, legumes, and occasional lean meats.

Feeding Guidelines

1. Pellets vs. Seed Mixes:

i. High-quality pellets formulated for parrots provide a balanced nutritional profile and help prevent selective eating.

ii. Limit seed mixes due to their high-fat content and potential for nutritional imbalances, offering as occasional treats.

2. Fresh Foods:

i. Offer fresh fruits and vegetables daily, washed thoroughly and cut into appropriate sizes.

ii. Rotate varieties to provide variety and ensure a wide range of nutrients.

3. Treats and Supplements:

i. Offer treats such as nuts, seeds (in moderation), and dried fruits sparingly.

ii. Use vitamin and mineral supplements only as recommended by an avian veterinarian to address specific deficiencies or during times of increased nutritional demand (e.g., breeding).

Hydration

1. Water Availability:

i. Provide fresh, clean water daily in a shallow dish or water bottle attached securely to the cage.

ii. Monitor water intake, especially during warmer months, to ensure adequate hydration.

Transitioning and Monitoring

1. Gradual Diet Changes:

i. Introduce new foods gradually to allow the bird to adjust and monitor for any digestive upset or aversion.

ii. Offer variety while ensuring a balanced diet to meet nutritional needs.

2. Monitoring Health and Body Condition:

i. Regularly observe your Pionus parrot for changes in appetite, weight, feather condition, and behavior.

ii. Consult an avian veterinarian if you notice any signs of nutritional deficiencies or health issues.

Meeting the essential nutritional needs of Pionus parrots is fundamental to their health and well-being. By offering a balanced diet that includes pellets, fresh fruits, vegetables, and occasional protein sources, you can provide your feathered companion with the nutrients needed for growth, energy, and immune function. Monitoring their diet, addressing potential deficiencies, and consulting with an avian veterinarian for guidance on specific nutritional requirements will help ensure a long and healthy life for your Pionus parrot. Investing in their dietary health contributes to their overall happiness and quality of life as a cherished member of your family.

4.2 Recommended Diet Plans and Feeding Schedule for Pionus Parrots

Establishing a well-balanced diet and a consistent feeding schedule is essential for maintaining the health, vitality, and overall well-being of Pionus parrots. These birds have specific dietary requirements that vary depending on factors such as age, activity level, and health status. By providing a variety of nutritious foods and following a structured feeding routine, you can ensure your Pionus parrot receives the essential nutrients needed for optimal health. Here's an extensive guide to recommended diet plans and feeding schedules for Pionus parrots:

Understanding Nutritional Needs

1. Balanced Diet Components:

A balanced diet for Pionus parrots should consist of the following components:

i. Pellets: High-quality pellets formulated specifically for parrots provide essential vitamins, minerals, and nutrients. Choose pellets that are free from artificial colors, flavors, and preservatives.

ii. Fresh Fruits and Vegetables: Offer a variety of fresh, bird-safe fruits and vegetables daily. These should include leafy greens (e.g., kale, spinach), carrots, sweet potatoes, bell peppers, berries, apples, and citrus fruits (in moderation).

iii. Whole Grains and Legumes: Incorporate cooked whole grains (e.g., brown rice, quinoa) and legumes (e.g., lentils, chickpeas) for added fiber, protein, and energy.

iv. Protein Sources: Provide occasional protein sources such as cooked lean meats (e.g., chicken, turkey), boiled eggs, or tofu. Avoid processed meats, fatty cuts, and excessive salt.

v. Nuts and Seeds: Offer small amounts of nuts (e.g., almonds, walnuts) and seeds (e.g., sunflower, pumpkin) as occasional treats due to their high-fat content.

2. Avoiding Toxic Foods:

i. Certain foods can be toxic to birds and should be avoided. These include chocolate, caffeine, avocado, alcohol, and foods with high salt or sugar content.

ii. Remove pits and seeds from fruits such as apples and cherries, as these can be toxic or pose a choking hazard.

Recommended Diet Plans

1. Pellet-Based Diet:

i. A pellet-based diet is recommended as the foundation of a Pionus parrot's daily nutrition.

ii. Offer high-quality pellets in a separate dish to ensure they are readily available throughout the day.

2. Fresh Foods:

i. Provide a variety of fresh fruits and vegetables, washed thoroughly and cut into appropriate sizes, daily.

ii. Rotate offerings to provide variety and ensure a wide range of nutrients. Monitor intake to prevent spoilage.

3. Cooked Foods:

i. Offer cooked whole grains, legumes, and occasional protein sources as part of their daily diet.

ii. Cooked foods should be prepared without added salt, oils, or seasonings that may be harmful to birds.

4. Treats:

i. Offer nuts, seeds, and dried fruits as occasional treats or rewards, limiting their intake due to their high-fat content.

Feeding Schedule

1. Daily Routine:

i. Establish a consistent feeding schedule based on your Pionus parrot's eating habits and preferences.

ii. Provide fresh water in a clean dish or water bottle daily, ensuring it is accessible at all times.

2. Morning Feeding:

i. Begin the day by offering fresh fruits and vegetables, supplemented with pellets.

ii. Allow your bird to eat freely from these offerings throughout the morning.

3. Midday Snack:

Provide a midday snack consisting of a small amount of fresh fruit or vegetables, encouraging foraging behavior.

4. Evening Meal:

i. Offer cooked grains, legumes, or a small amount of protein source (e.g., boiled egg, cooked chicken) in the evening.

ii. Monitor intake to prevent overfeeding and remove uneaten food to maintain cleanliness.

5. Treats and Supplements:

i. Offer nuts, seeds, or dried fruits as occasional treats, limiting their quantity to maintain a balanced diet.

ii. Use vitamin and mineral supplements only as recommended by an avian veterinarian to address specific deficiencies or during periods of increased nutritional demand (e.g., breeding season).

Transitioning and Monitoring

1. Gradual Introductions:

i. Introduce new foods gradually to allow your Pionus parrot to adjust to different tastes and textures.

ii. Monitor for any signs of digestive upset or aversion and adjust offerings accordingly.

2. Monitoring Health:

i. Regularly monitor your Pionus parrot's health, including weight, feather condition, droppings, and overall behavior.

ii. Consult an avian veterinarian if you notice any changes in appetite, energy levels, or signs of nutritional deficiencies.

Hydration

1. Water Availability:

i. Provide fresh, clean water daily in a shallow dish or water bottle attached securely to the cage.

ii. Monitor water intake to ensure your Pionus parrot remains adequately hydrated, especially during warmer months.

Providing a well-balanced diet and establishing a consistent feeding schedule are essential for the health and happiness of Pionus parrots. By offering a variety of pellets, fresh fruits, vegetables, whole grains, and occasional protein sources, you can meet their nutritional needs and ensure they receive essential vitamins, minerals, and nutrients. Monitoring their diet, avoiding toxic foods, and offering treats in moderation contribute to their overall well-being and longevity as cherished members of your family. Regular veterinary check-ups and adjustments to their diet as needed will help maintain optimal health and ensure a fulfilling life for your Pionus parrot.

4.3 Handling Treats and Supplements for Pionus Parrots

Treats and supplements play a significant role in the diet and overall well-being of Pionus parrots. While treats can be used to provide variety and enrichment, supplements are essential for addressing specific nutritional needs or deficiencies. However, it's crucial to handle treats and supplements with care to ensure they enhance your parrot's health without causing harm. Here's an extensive guide on handling treats and supplements for Pionus parrots:

Understanding Treats for Pionus Parrots

1. Purpose of Treats:

i. Treats serve as rewards for good behavior, training incentives, and sources of additional nutrients.

ii. They provide variety in taste and texture, stimulating foraging behavior and mental engagement.

2. Types of Treats:

i. Nut Treats: Offer small amounts of nuts such as almonds, walnuts, and pecans as occasional treats due to their high-fat content.

ii. Seed Treats: Provide seeds like sunflower or pumpkin seeds sparingly to prevent nutritional imbalances.

iii. Dried Fruits: Offer dried fruits such as raisins, cranberries, or apricots in moderation as they are concentrated in sugars.

3. Healthy Treat Options:

i. Choose treats that are low in salt, sugar, and additives.

ii. Opt for organic or unsweetened varieties when possible to minimize unnecessary additives.

Guidelines for Offering Treats

1. Moderation:

i. Offer treats sparingly to prevent overconsumption and maintain a balanced diet.

ii. Limit treats to no more than 10% of your Pionus parrot's total daily food intake.

2. Variety:

i. Rotate treats to provide variety and prevent boredom.

ii. Offer different types of treats in small quantities to gauge your bird's preferences.

3. Foraging Opportunities:

i. Incorporate treats into foraging toys or puzzles to encourage natural behaviors and mental stimulation.

ii. This helps promote physical activity and keeps your parrot engaged.

Handling Supplements

1. Purpose of Supplements:

i. Supplements are used to address specific nutritional deficiencies, support health during certain life stages (e.g., breeding, molting), or enhance overall well-being.

ii. They should only be used under the guidance of an avian veterinarian to ensure they are appropriate and necessary for your parrot.

2. Types of Supplements:

i. Vitamin Supplements: Provide additional vitamins (e.g., vitamin A, D3) when dietary sources are insufficient.

ii. Mineral Supplements: Offer calcium supplements to support bone health and eggshell formation (for breeding females).

iii. Probiotics: Maintain gut health and digestion, especially during periods of stress or antibiotic treatment.

3. Dosage and Administration:

i. Follow dosage instructions provided by your avian veterinarian carefully.

ii. Administer supplements directly into your parrot's food, water, or orally, ensuring they are consumed as directed.

Choosing Quality Products

1. Read Labels:

i. Select treats and supplements that are specifically formulated for parrots.

ii. Read ingredient labels to avoid products containing artificial colors, flavors, preservatives, or harmful additives.

2. Consult Your Veterinarian:

i. Seek guidance from an avian veterinarian before introducing new treats or supplements to your parrot's diet.

ii. They can recommend suitable products based on your bird's age, health status, and nutritional needs.

Monitoring and Adjustments

1. Observational Monitoring:

i. Watch for any changes in your parrot's behavior, appetite, droppings, or overall health after introducing treats or supplements.

ii. Discontinue use and consult your veterinarian if you notice any adverse reactions or concerns.

2. Adjustments as Needed:

i. Modify treat and supplement offerings based on your parrot's response and health status.

ii. Regularly review your bird's diet and make adjustments to ensure they receive optimal nutrition.

Handling treats and supplements responsibly is crucial for maintaining the health and well-being of Pionus parrots. By offering treats in moderation, providing a variety of healthy options, and incorporating supplements under veterinary guidance, you can enhance your parrot's diet and overall quality of life. Monitoring their diet, observing for any changes, and consulting with an avian veterinarian as needed will help ensure that treats and supplements contribute positively to your Pionus parrot's nutritional needs and enjoyment. With careful management, treats and supplements can be valuable tools in promoting a balanced and fulfilling diet for your feathered companion.

CHAPTER FIVE

Health and Veterinary Care

5.1 Signs of a Healthy Pionus Parrot

Recognizing signs of a healthy Pionus parrot is essential for proactive avian care and ensuring your feathered companion's well-being. By regularly monitoring their physical appearance, behavior, and overall condition, you can detect any potential health concerns early and take appropriate action. Here's an extensive guide on the signs of a healthy Pionus parrot:

Physical Signs

1. Feathers:

i. Feathers should be smooth, glossy, and well-groomed without signs of fluffiness or ruffled appearance.

ii. There should be no bald patches, plucked feathers, or uneven molting patterns, which could indicate stress, illness, or poor nutrition.

2. Eyes:

i. Eyes should be bright, clear, and free from discharge or swelling.

ii. The parrot's eyes should be alert and responsive to its surroundings.

3. Beak and Nails:

i. The beak should be smooth, without cracks or discoloration, and the nails should be well-trimmed.

ii. Beak and nail growth should be moderate and not excessively long.

4. Skin and Plumage:

i. Skin around the face, legs, and feet should be smooth and free from lesions, redness, or flaking.

ii. Plumage should be vibrant in coloration, indicating good overall health and proper nutrition.

Behavioral Signs

1. Activity Level:

i. A healthy Pionus parrot will be active and engaged in its environment, showing curiosity and interest in surroundings.

ii. Engages in normal playful behaviors such as climbing, exploring toys, and vocalizing.

2. Appetite and Eating Habits:

i. Maintains a regular appetite and shows enthusiasm for eating a variety of foods.

ii. Drinks water regularly throughout the day, keeping hydrated.

3. Vocalizations:

Exhibits a range of vocalizations appropriate to its species, expressing contentment, curiosity, and communication with its environment.

General Health Indicators

1. Respiratory Health:

Breathing should be quiet, steady, and without any wheezing, clicking, or audible respiratory distress.

2. Droppings:

i. Droppings should be well-formed, with distinct components (feces, urine, urates), and without unusual color, odor, or consistency changes.

ii. The frequency of droppings should be consistent, indicating a healthy digestive system.

Social Interaction

1. Bonding and Trust:

i. Shows trust and affection towards its human caregivers, willingly stepping up and seeking interaction.

ii. Enjoys social interaction with humans and other household members.

Veterinary Check-ups

1. Regular Check-ups:

i. Regular veterinary check-ups are essential for preventive care and monitoring your Pionus parrot's health status.

ii. Consult with an avian veterinarian if you notice any changes in behavior, appetite, or physical appearance that may indicate illness or discomfort.

Environmental Factors

1. Optimal Environment:

i. Lives in a clean, well-maintained environment with appropriate temperature, humidity, and lighting conditions.

ii. Receives mental stimulation and enrichment through toys, foraging activities, and interaction with caregivers.

Monitoring the signs of a healthy Pionus parrot involves regular observation of their physical appearance, behavior, appetite, and interaction with their environment. By understanding these indicators and maintaining a proactive approach to avian care, you can promote your parrot's well-being and detect any potential health issues early. Establishing a trusting relationship with your avian veterinarian and seeking guidance as needed will ensure that your Pionus parrot enjoys a long, healthy, and fulfilling life as a cherished companion in your home.

5.2 Common Health Issues and Preventative Care for Pionus Parrots

Ensuring the health and well-being of Pionus parrots involves understanding common health issues they may face and implementing effective preventative care strategies. By being aware of potential health concerns, practicing good husbandry, providing a balanced diet, and scheduling regular veterinary check-ups, you can significantly reduce the risk of illnesses and promote a long, healthy life for your feathered companion. Here's a comprehensive overview of common health issues and preventative care for Pionus parrots:

Common Health Issues

1. Respiratory Problems:

Symptoms: Signs of respiratory issues may include sneezing, nasal discharge, wheezing, labored breathing, or clicking sounds while breathing.

Causes: Respiratory infections can be caused by bacteria, viruses, fungi, or environmental factors such as drafts or poor ventilation.

Prevention: Ensure a clean and well-ventilated environment. Avoid exposure to cigarette smoke, aerosol sprays, or strong fumes.

2. Nutritional Deficiencies:

Symptoms: Signs of nutritional deficiencies may include feather abnormalities, poor growth, lethargy, or changes in appetite.

Causes: Inadequate diet lacking essential vitamins (e.g., vitamin A, D3), minerals (e.g., calcium), or protein.

Prevention: Provide a balanced diet consisting of pellets, fresh fruits, vegetables, and occasional protein sources. Monitor for signs of deficiency and supplement as directed by a veterinarian.

3. Gastrointestinal Disorders:

Symptoms: Symptoms of gastrointestinal issues include diarrhea, changes in droppings (color, consistency), vomiting, or loss of appetite.

Causes: Dietary indiscretions (e.g., eating toxic plants), bacterial infections, parasites (e.g., worms), or stress.

Prevention: Offer a variety of fresh, clean foods and avoid feeding toxic or spoiled foods. Maintain a clean cage and provide regular opportunities for exercise and mental stimulation.

4. Feather Plucking and Self-Mutilation:

Symptoms: Self-mutilation behaviors include feather plucking, excessive grooming, or biting at skin.

Causes: Stress, boredom, medical conditions (e.g., skin infections, parasites), or environmental factors.

Prevention: Address underlying causes of stress or boredom through enrichment activities, social interaction, and maintaining a stable environment.

5. Avian Papilloma Virus (APV):

Symptoms: APV may present as growths or lesions on the skin, beak, or inside the mouth.

Causes: Viral infection transmitted through contact with infected birds or contaminated objects.

Prevention: Practice strict quarantine measures for new birds, maintain good hygiene, and avoid sharing toys or perches between birds of unknown health status.

6. Psittacosis (Chlamydiosis):

Symptoms: Signs of psittacosis include respiratory distress, lethargy, weight loss, nasal discharge, or eye infections.

Causes: Bacterial infection (Chlamydia psittaci) transmitted through inhalation of contaminated dust or direct contact with infected birds.

Prevention: Quarantine new birds, maintain good hygiene, and seek immediate veterinary care for any suspected cases.

Preventative Care Practices

1. Veterinary Check-ups:

i. Establish a regular veterinary check-up schedule (at least annually) with an avian veterinarian experienced in treating parrots.

ii. Routine physical examinations, fecal screenings, and blood tests can detect early signs of illness or nutritional deficiencies.

2. Diet and Nutrition:

i. Provide a balanced diet consisting of high-quality pellets, fresh fruits, vegetables, and occasional protein sources.

ii. Offer vitamin and mineral supplements as recommended by a veterinarian to address specific nutritional needs.

3. Environmental Management:

i. Maintain a clean cage environment, regularly removing droppings, and providing fresh water daily.

ii. Ensure stable temperature (65-80°F or 18-27°C) and humidity levels (40-70%) within the parrot's habitat.

4. Behavioral Enrichment:

i. Offer a variety of toys, puzzles, and foraging opportunities to stimulate mental and physical activity.

ii. Engage in regular social interaction with your parrot to prevent boredom and promote mental well-being.

5. Quarantine and Biosecurity:

i. Quarantine new birds for at least 30 days before introducing them to existing flock members.

ii. Practice good hygiene, including handwashing before and after handling birds or cleaning cages, to prevent the spread of disease.

6. Emergency Preparedness:

i. Familiarize yourself with common signs of illness and emergency veterinary contact information.

ii. Maintain a first aid kit with essential supplies for treating minor injuries or health emergencies.

7. Observational Monitoring:

i. Monitor your Pionus parrot daily for any changes in behavior, appetite, droppings, or physical appearance.

ii. Promptly address any abnormalities or concerns by seeking veterinary advice.

By understanding common health issues, practicing preventative care measures, and maintaining a vigilant approach to monitoring your Pionus parrot's health, you can provide them with a safe, nurturing environment conducive to their well-being. Establishing a relationship with an avian veterinarian, implementing a balanced diet, ensuring environmental enrichment, and practicing good hygiene are essential steps in promoting a healthy and fulfilling life for your feathered companion. With proactive care and attention to their needs, you can help your Pionus parrot thrive and enjoy a long-lasting bond as part of your family.

5.3 Finding a Qualified Avian Veterinarian

Finding a qualified avian veterinarian is crucial for ensuring the health, well-being, and longevity of your Pionus parrot. Avian veterinarians specialize in the care and treatment of birds, including parrots, and possess the knowledge, experience, and resources necessary to provide comprehensive medical care. Here's a comprehensive guide on how to find and choose a qualified avian veterinarian for your Pionus parrot:

Importance of Avian Veterinarians

1. Specialized Knowledge:

Avian veterinarians have specialized training in the unique anatomy, physiology, and behavior of birds, including parrots like Pionus parrots. They are equipped to diagnose and treat avian-specific health issues and provide preventive care tailored to the needs of birds.

2. Diagnostic Tools and Techniques:

Avian veterinarians utilize specialized diagnostic tools and techniques, such as endoscopy, radiography, blood tests, and microbiological cultures, to assess and monitor bird health. They have access to avian-specific medications and treatments to address medical conditions effectively.

3. Preventive Care Expertise:

Avian veterinarians emphasize preventive care, including routine health exams, vaccinations, parasite control, and nutritional counseling, to maintain bird health and detect early signs of illness.

How to Find a Qualified Avian Veterinarian

1. Recommendations:

i. Local Avicultural Societies: Contact local avicultural societies, bird clubs, or breeders' associations for recommendations on avian veterinarians in your area.

ii. Pet Owners: Ask fellow parrot owners or enthusiasts for their experiences and recommendations for avian veterinarians they trust.

2. Veterinary Directories:

i. Association Websites: Check websites of professional associations such as the Association of Avian Veterinarians (AAV) or American Veterinary Medical Association (AVMA) for directories of accredited avian veterinarians.

ii. Online Reviews: Look for online reviews and testimonials from pet owners to gauge the reputation and quality of care provided by avian veterinarians.

3. Consultation and Visit:

i. Initial Consultation: Schedule an initial consultation or visit with the avian veterinarian to discuss their experience, qualifications, and approach to avian care.

ii. Facility Inspection: Evaluate the veterinary clinic or hospital for cleanliness, avian-specific equipment, and the presence of experienced staff familiar with avian handling.

Qualities to Look for in an Avian Veterinarian

1. Avian Experience:

i. Choose an avian veterinarian with significant experience in treating parrots and other birds.

ii. Inquire about their caseload of avian patients and the types of avian species they regularly treat.

2. Education and Credentials:

i. Verify the veterinarian's education, training, and credentials, including board certification in avian practice if applicable.

ii. Look for memberships in professional organizations such as the AAV or AVMA, indicating a commitment to continuing education and high standards of avian care.

3. Communication and Approach:

i. Seek a veterinarian who communicates effectively and listens to your concerns about your Pionus parrot's health.

ii. Ensure they provide clear explanations of diagnoses, treatment options, and preventive care recommendations tailored to your bird's specific needs.

4. Emergency Care Availability:

i. Inquire about emergency care availability, including after-hours services or referrals to emergency clinics for avian emergencies.

ii. Know the procedures for contacting the veterinarian in case of urgent health issues outside regular business hours.

Building a Relationship with Your Avian Veterinarian

1. Regular Check-ups:

i. Schedule regular wellness exams for your Pionus parrot to monitor their health and detect early signs of illness.

ii. Discuss vaccination schedules, parasite prevention, and nutritional guidelines with your avian veterinarian.

2. Health Maintenance Plan:

i. Work with your avian veterinarian to develop a customized health maintenance plan based on your parrot's age, health history, and environmental factors.

ii. Follow recommendations for diet, enrichment, and hygiene practices to promote optimal health and well-being.

3. Trust and Communication:

i. Foster a trusting relationship with your avian veterinarian based on open communication, mutual respect, and collaborative decision-making regarding your parrot's care.

ii. Keep your veterinarian informed of any changes in your parrot's behavior, appetite, or physical condition promptly.

Finding a qualified avian veterinarian is essential for providing the best possible care for your Pionus parrot. By conducting research, seeking recommendations, and evaluating credentials and experience, you can select a veterinarian who meets your parrot's unique health needs. Building a positive relationship with your avian veterinarian, scheduling regular check-ups, and following preventive care guidelines will help ensure your Pionus parrot enjoys a healthy and fulfilling life as a cherished companion in your home.

CHAPTER SIX

Training and Enrichment

6.1 Basics of Training Your Pionus Parrot

Training your Pionus parrot is an enriching experience that enhances the bond between you and your feathered companion while promoting mental stimulation and positive behavior. Whether you're teaching basic commands, socializing your parrot, or addressing specific behavioral issues, understanding the fundamentals of training is essential for successful and rewarding interactions. Here's a comprehensive guide to the basics of training your Pionus parrot:

Importance of Training

1. Bonding and Trust:

Training strengthens the bond between you and your Pionus parrot through positive reinforcement and mutual interaction. It builds trust and encourages socialization, fostering a harmonious relationship based on communication and understanding.

2. Mental Stimulation:

Training provides mental enrichment and prevents boredom by engaging your parrot's cognitive abilities. It promotes problem-solving skills and encourages natural behaviors, enhancing overall mental well-being.

3. Behavioral Management:

Training helps address and modify undesirable behaviors such as aggression, biting, or excessive vocalization. It establishes clear boundaries and encourages desirable behaviors through consistent reinforcement.

Getting Started with Training

1. Establishing Trust:

i. Build trust and familiarity with your Pionus parrot through gentle handling, positive interactions, and respecting their comfort zones.

ii. Use a calm and reassuring voice to communicate during training sessions.

2. Setting Training Goals:

i. Define clear, achievable goals for training sessions, focusing on one behavior or command at a time.

ii. Start with simple tasks before progressing to more complex behaviors, ensuring success and reinforcement along the way.

3. Timing and Consistency:

i. Conduct training sessions in short, frequent intervals (5-10 minutes) throughout the day to maintain your parrot's focus and interest.

ii. Be consistent in your training approach, using the same cues, rewards, and techniques to reinforce desired behaviors.

Positive Reinforcement Techniques

1. Reward-Based Training:

i. Use positive reinforcement, such as favorite treats, praise, or affectionate gestures, to reward your parrot for performing desired behaviors.

ii. Timing is crucial; reward immediately after the desired behavior to reinforce the connection between action and reward.

2. Clicker Training:

i. Incorporate a clicker as a conditioned reinforcer, pairing the click sound with treats to mark and reinforce desired behaviors effectively.

ii. Clicker training helps clarify communication and signals to your parrot when they have performed correctly.

3. Patience and Persistence:

i. Remain patient and persistent during training, understanding that each parrot learns at its own pace.

ii. Avoid punishment or negative reinforcement, as it can undermine trust and lead to fear-based behaviors.

Basic Training Commands

1. Step-Up Command:

i. Teach your Pionus parrot to step onto your hand or a perch on command ("Step up") using positive reinforcement and gentle encouragement.

ii. Gradually increase the distance and duration of stepping up exercises to build confidence and trust.

2. Target Training:

i. Introduce target training by presenting a handheld target stick or object for your parrot to touch with its beak ("Touch").

ii. Reward each touch with a treat, gradually shaping the behavior to follow the target and move in different directions.

3. Recall Training:

i. Teach recall ("Come" or "Here") by calling your parrot from a short distance and rewarding them generously upon compliance.

ii. Practice in a safe, enclosed environment to prevent flight accidents and reinforce the behavior with positive experiences.

Addressing Behavioral Issues

1. Understanding Behavior:

i. Identify and understand the underlying causes of behavioral issues, such as fear, boredom, or lack of socialization.

ii. Modify the environment and routines to address triggers and promote positive behaviors.

2. Desensitization and Counterconditioning:

i. Use desensitization techniques to gradually expose your parrot to feared objects or situations, pairing them with positive experiences (counterconditioning).

ii. Break down tasks into manageable steps, rewarding calm behavior and gradually increasing exposure to challenging stimuli.

Consistency and Long-Term Training

1. Consistent Reinforcement:

i. Maintain consistent reinforcement of trained behaviors through regular practice and occasional refresher sessions.

ii. Review previously learned commands and behaviors to reinforce reliability and prevent regression.

2. Long-Term Engagement:

i. Keep training sessions engaging and varied to prevent boredom and maintain your parrot's interest.

ii. Introduce new challenges, tricks, or games to stimulate mental agility and continue building a strong bond.

Training your Pionus parrot is a rewarding journey that fosters communication, trust, and mental stimulation. By understanding the basics of training, using positive reinforcement techniques, and addressing behavioral issues with patience and consistency, you can create a positive learning environment for your parrot. Building a strong foundation of trust and mutual respect through training strengthens your bond and enhances the overall well-being of your Pionus parrot, enriching both of your lives as companions.

6.2 Socialization and Bonding Techniques for Pionus Parrots

Socialization and bonding are crucial aspects of caring for a Pionus parrot, as they promote trust, confidence, and a positive relationship between you and your feathered companion. These techniques focus on creating a secure and stimulating environment that encourages social interaction, mental stimulation, and emotional well-being. Here's a comprehensive guide to socialization and bonding techniques for Pionus parrots:

Importance of Socialization

1. Relationship Building:

i. Socialization strengthens the bond between you and your Pionus parrot, fostering trust and companionship.

ii. It enhances mutual understanding and communication, enriching your interactions and promoting a harmonious relationship.

2. Emotional Well-being:

i. Socialization provides mental stimulation and prevents boredom, reducing the risk of behavioral issues such as aggression or feather plucking.

ii. It promotes emotional health by fulfilling your parrot's social and psychological needs for companionship and interaction.

Techniques for Socialization

1. Positive Interaction:

i. Gentle Handling: Approach your Pionus parrot calmly and respectfully, using slow movements and gentle touches to build trust.

ii. Verbal Communication: Talk to your parrot in a soothing voice to reassure them and establish a positive association with your presence.

2. Physical Contact:

i. Step-Up Training: Teach your parrot to step onto your hand or a perch ("Step up"), gradually increasing physical contact and handling.

ii. Head Scratches: Offer gentle head scratches or neck rubs as your parrot becomes comfortable with physical touch.

3. Play and Enrichment:

i. Interactive Toys: Provide a variety of safe, stimulating toys such as puzzles, foraging toys, and chewable items to encourage play and exploration.

ii. Games: Engage in interactive games such as peek-a-boo, hide-and-seek, or object retrieval to promote mental agility and bonding.

4. Out-of-Cage Time:

i. Supervised Freedom: Allow supervised out-of-cage time in a safe, bird-proofed area to promote exercise, exploration, and social interaction.

ii. Training Sessions: Use out-of-cage time for training exercises, encouraging positive behaviors and reinforcing obedience.

Building Trust

1. Patience and Consistency:

i. Build trust gradually through patient and consistent interactions, respecting your parrot's pace and comfort level.

ii. Establish predictable routines and positive reinforcement to create a sense of security and reliability.

2. Respect Boundaries:

i. Recognize and respect your parrot's body language and signals, such as vocalizations or posture changes, indicating comfort or discomfort.

ii. Avoid forcing interactions or handling when your parrot shows signs of stress or reluctance.

Bonding Techniques

1. Quality Time Together:

i. Spend dedicated, uninterrupted time with your Pionus parrot daily, engaging in activities that promote interaction and bonding.

ii. Create a bond-building routine, such as morning greetings, mealtime interactions, or bedtime rituals, to strengthen your relationship.

2. Mutual Activities:

i. Share activities that your parrot enjoys, such as exploring new toys, foraging for treats, or participating in training sessions.

ii. Participate in activities that promote physical closeness and shared experiences, reinforcing the bond between you and your parrot.

Addressing Behavioral Challenges

1. Positive Reinforcement:

i. Use positive reinforcement techniques to encourage desired behaviors, such as offering treats or praise for calm behavior or compliance with commands.

ii. Redirect undesirable behaviors through alternative activities or commands, avoiding punishment or negative reinforcement.

2. Consistent Boundaries:

i. Establish consistent boundaries and rules for interaction to reinforce acceptable behaviors and prevent reinforcement of undesirable habits.

ii. Communicate expectations clearly through training and consistent reinforcement of positive behaviors.

Monitoring and Adjustments

1. Observational Awareness:

i. Monitor your Pionus parrot's behavior, appetite, and physical condition for any signs of stress, discomfort, or changes in behavior.

ii. Address concerns promptly by adjusting socialization techniques or seeking veterinary advice if behavioral issues persist.

2. Long-Term Engagement:

i. Maintain ongoing socialization and bonding efforts throughout your parrot's life, adapting activities and interactions to meet evolving needs.

ii. Continue to nurture your relationship through regular enrichment, positive reinforcement, and quality time together.

Socialization and bonding techniques are essential for nurturing a positive and fulfilling relationship with your Pionus parrot. By using gentle handling, positive reinforcement, and engaging enrichment activities, you can promote trust, companionship, and mental well-being. Building a strong bond through mutual respect, patience, and consistent interaction enhances the quality of life for both you and your parrot, creating a rewarding and harmonious companionship that lasts a lifetime.

6.3 Enrichment Activities and Toys for Pionus Parrots

Enrichment activities and toys play a crucial role in enhancing the physical, mental, and emotional well-being of Pionus parrots. These activities stimulate natural behaviors, prevent boredom, and provide mental enrichment, promoting a healthy and fulfilling life for your feathered companion. Here's a comprehensive guide to enrichment activities and toys for Pionus parrots:

Importance of Enrichment

1. Mental Stimulation:

i. Enrichment activities challenge your Pionus parrot's cognitive abilities, preventing boredom and encouraging problem-solving skills.

ii. They stimulate curiosity and exploration, promoting mental agility and overall mental well-being.

2. Physical Exercise:

i. Active enrichment activities, such as climbing, foraging, and playing with toys, promote physical exercise and maintain your parrot's physical health.

ii. They help prevent obesity and muscle atrophy by encouraging movement and activity.

3. Behavioral Health:

i. Enrichment reduces stress and anxiety by providing outlets for natural behaviors, such as chewing, exploring, and social interaction.

ii. It minimizes boredom-related behaviors, such as feather picking or excessive vocalization, promoting a calm and contented demeanor.

Types of Enrichment Activities

1. Foraging Activities:

i. Puzzle Feeders: Provide puzzle feeders or foraging toys that require your parrot to manipulate objects or solve puzzles to access food.

ii. Scatter Feeding: Scatter food or treats in different areas of the cage or play area to encourage natural foraging behaviors.

2. Chew Toys and Shreddables:

i. Natural Wood Toys: Offer untreated, bird-safe wood blocks, branches, or chew toys that allow your parrot to chew and shred.

ii. Paper-based Toys: Provide paper-based toys or cardboard rolls for shredding, which satisfies natural chewing and nesting instincts.

3. Climbing and Perching:

i. Play Gyms: Set up play gyms or climbing structures with varying levels, ropes, ladders, and perches to encourage physical exercise and exploration.

ii. Swings and Perches: Rotate different types of perches and swings regularly to provide variety and stimulate balance and coordination.

4. Interactive Toys:

i. Noise-Making Toys: Offer bells, rattles, or toys that make noise to engage your parrot's auditory senses and encourage interaction.

ii. Interactive Puzzles: Use interactive toys or games that require your parrot to manipulate objects, such as pushing buttons or turning knobs.

5. Environmental Variety:

i. Rotation of Toys: Rotate toys regularly to maintain novelty and prevent habituation, keeping your parrot interested and engaged.

ii. Natural Elements: Introduce natural elements such as branches, leaves, or safe plants (non-toxic) to mimic natural environments and provide sensory stimulation.

Creating a Stimulating Environment

1. Cage Setup:

i. Spacious Environment: Provide a spacious cage with room for toys, perches, and activities that allow your parrot to move freely and explore.

ii. Safe Placement: Ensure toys are securely attached and placed away from food and water bowls to prevent contamination.

2. Out-of-Cage Time:

i. Supervised Exploration: Allow supervised out-of-cage time in a bird-proofed area to explore, interact with toys, and engage in natural behaviors.

ii. Training and Play: Use out-of-cage time for training sessions, playtime, or social interaction to further enrich your parrot's experience.

3. Variety and Rotation:

i. Introduce a variety of toys and enrichment activities to cater to different interests and preferences, keeping your parrot engaged and stimulated.

ii. Rotate toys regularly to maintain interest and prevent boredom, introducing new challenges and experiences over time.

Tailoring Enrichment to Individual Needs

i. Observation and Adjustment: Observe your parrot's preferences and responses to different toys and activities, adjusting enrichment strategies accordingly.

ii. Customization: Tailor enrichment activities to your parrot's age, health, and personality traits to ensure relevance and enjoyment.

Enrichment activities and toys are essential for promoting the overall health, happiness, and well-being of Pionus parrots. By providing a stimulating environment that encourages natural behaviors, physical exercise, and mental engagement, you enhance your parrot's quality of life and strengthen your bond.

Incorporate a variety of enrichment activities, monitor for safety, and observe your parrot's responses to tailor enrichment to their individual needs. With thoughtful planning and creativity, you can create a dynamic and enriching environment that supports your Pionus parrot's holistic health and happiness.

CHAPTER SEVEN

Behavioral Insights and Challenges

7.1 Understanding Pionus Parrot Behavior Cues

Understanding Pionus parrot behavior cues is essential for interpreting their emotions, needs, and communication signals effectively. By recognizing and responding to these cues, you can foster a positive relationship with your parrot and address their physical and psychological well-being. Here's a comprehensive guide to understanding Pionus parrot behavior cues:

Importance of Understanding Behavior Cues

1. Communication:

Behavior cues serve as a primary means of communication for Pionus parrots, allowing them to express emotions, needs, and intentions. Understanding these cues promotes effective interaction and enhances mutual understanding between you and your parrot.

2. Welfare and Well-being:

Recognizing behavior cues helps identify signs of stress, discomfort, or illness, enabling prompt intervention and appropriate care. It supports the provision of a stimulating environment and tailored care that promotes your parrot's physical and psychological welfare.

Common Behavior Cues

1. Body Language:

i. Feather Position: Fluffed feathers indicate relaxation or contentment, while flattened feathers against the body may signal fear or aggression.

ii. Posture: Upright posture with raised crest suggests alertness or curiosity, whereas a lowered posture may indicate submission or discomfort.

2. Vocalizations:

i. Tones and Pitch: Different vocal tones and pitches convey various emotions, such as excitement, contentment, alarm, or distress.

ii. Specific Calls: Pionus parrots may have specific vocalizations for greeting, warning, seeking attention, or expressing discomfort.

3. Eye and Beak Movements:

i. Dilated Pupils: Dilated pupils can indicate excitement or arousal, while pinpoint pupils may suggest fear or stress.

ii. Beak Clacking or Grinding: Beak clacking may signal contentment or anticipation, while grinding may indicate relaxation or comfort.

4. Feeding and Eating Behavior:

i. Appetite Changes: Changes in appetite or feeding behavior may indicate health issues, stress, or dietary preferences.

ii. Foraging Behavior: Active foraging or exploring food items can signify engagement and mental stimulation.

5. Social Interactions:

i. Greeting Behaviors: Head bobbing, tail wagging, or vocal greetings may indicate social interaction and bonding.

ii. Aggression: Aggressive behavior, such as lunging, biting, or raised feathers, signals discomfort, fear, or territoriality.

Interpreting Behavior Cues

1. Context and Environment:

i. Consider the context and environmental factors influencing your parrot's behavior, such as changes in routine, presence of visitors, or new stimuli.

ii. Observe behavior cues in various situations to gain a comprehensive understanding of your parrot's responses and needs.

2. Individual Variation:

i. Recognize that behavior cues may vary among individual Pionus parrots based on personality, past experiences, and socialization history.

ii. Tailor your interpretation and response to align with your parrot's unique behaviors and communication style.

Responding to Behavior Cues

1. Positive Reinforcement:

i. Use positive reinforcement, such as treats, praise, or affection, to reinforce desirable behaviors and encourage trust and cooperation.

ii. Reward calm, responsive behavior to reinforce positive interactions and foster a supportive environment.

2. Addressing Concerns:

i. Promptly address behavior cues indicating stress, fear, or discomfort by providing reassurance, removing potential stressors, or adjusting the environment.

ii. Consult with an avian veterinarian if behavior cues persist or indicate underlying health issues requiring medical attention.

Building Trust and Relationship

1. Patience and Consistency:

i. Build trust and strengthen your relationship with your Pionus parrot through patient, consistent responses to behavior cues.

ii. Establish predictable routines and interactions that promote security and reliability in your parrot's environment.

2. Observation and Learning:

i. Continuously observe and learn from your parrot's behavior cues to refine your understanding and responsiveness over time.

ii. Invest in ongoing socialization, enrichment, and positive reinforcement to nurture a harmonious bond based on mutual trust and respect.

Understanding Pionus parrot behavior cues is fundamental to fostering effective communication, promoting well-being, and nurturing a fulfilling relationship with your feathered companion. By interpreting body language, vocalizations, and other behavior cues, you can respond appropriately to their emotional and physical needs, enhancing their quality of life and strengthening your bond. Through observation, patience, and tailored care, you can create a supportive environment that supports your Pionus parrot's natural behaviors and ensures their overall health and happiness.

7.2 Addressing Common Behavioral Issues in Pionus Parrots

Addressing common behavioral issues in Pionus parrots is crucial for promoting their well-being and maintaining a harmonious relationship between you and your feathered companion. By understanding the underlying causes and employing appropriate strategies, you can effectively manage and resolve behavioral challenges. Here's a comprehensive guide to addressing common behavioral issues in Pionus parrots:

Common Behavioral Issues

1. Biting and Aggression:

Causes: Biting and aggression can stem from fear, territoriality, hormonal changes, stress, or lack of socialization.

Strategies: Implement positive reinforcement, avoid triggering situations, use distraction techniques, and gradually desensitize your parrot to potential stressors.

2. Screaming and Vocalizations:

Causes: Excessive vocalizations may result from attention-seeking, territorial behavior, boredom, or communication needs.

Strategies: Provide mental stimulation, establish a routine, reinforce quiet behavior, and address underlying reasons through environmental enrichment and positive reinforcement.

3. Feather Plucking and Self-Mutilation:

Causes: Feather plucking and self-mutilation can indicate stress, boredom, health issues, or psychological distress.

Strategies: Identify and address underlying causes, such as environmental stressors or medical conditions, provide enrichment activities, and consult with a veterinarian for a comprehensive health assessment.

4. Fear and Shyness:

Causes: Fear and shyness may arise from lack of socialization, past negative experiences, or changes in environment.

Strategies: Build trust through positive reinforcement, gradual exposure to new stimuli, and patience in interactions to reduce fear and encourage confidence.

5. Destructive Behavior:

Causes: Destructive behavior, such as chewing on furniture or cage bars, may result from boredom, lack of enrichment, or hormonal changes.

Strategies: Provide appropriate chew toys, rotate toys regularly, increase mental stimulation through foraging activities, and redirect destructive behavior positively.

6. Jealousy and Attention-Seeking:

Causes: Jealousy and attention-seeking behaviors can develop in response to perceived competition for attention or changes in routine.

Strategies: Reinforce positive behaviors, maintain consistent interactions, and ensure each parrot receives individual attention and enrichment to prevent jealousy.

Approaches to Addressing Behavioral Issues

1. Positive Reinforcement:

Use positive reinforcement techniques, such as treats, praise, or favorite toys, to reward desirable behaviors and encourage cooperation.

2. Environmental Enrichment:

Provide a stimulating environment with varied toys, perches, and activities that cater to natural behaviors and prevent boredom.

3. Consistency and Routine:

Establish consistent routines for feeding, socialization, and playtime to promote stability and reduce stress.

4. Behavioral Modification:

Employ behavior modification techniques, such as desensitization and counterconditioning, to address fear-based behaviors gradually.

5. Veterinary Consultation:

Consult with an avian veterinarian to rule out underlying health issues contributing to behavioral problems and develop a holistic treatment plan.

Tips for Addressing Behavioral Issues

1. Observation and Understanding:

Observe your Pionus parrot's behavior cues to identify triggers and patterns influencing behavioral issues.

2. Patience and Persistence:

Address behavioral issues with patience and persistence, understanding that changes may take time and consistent effort.

3. Avoid Punishment:

Avoid punishment or negative reinforcement, as it can increase stress and worsen behavioral problems in parrots.

4. Seek Professional Guidance:

Seek guidance from avian behaviorists or experienced aviculturists for specialized advice on managing complex behavioral issues.

Building a Positive Relationship

1. Trust and Bonding:

Build trust through positive interactions, respect for boundaries, and attentive care to strengthen your relationship with your parrot.

2. Communication and Understanding:

Foster communication through understanding behavior cues, responsive care, and proactive management of your parrot's needs.

Addressing common behavioral issues in Pionus parrots requires a proactive approach that emphasizes understanding, patience, and tailored strategies. By identifying underlying causes, implementing positive reinforcement, providing enrichment, and seeking professional guidance when needed, you can effectively manage and resolve behavioral challenges. Building a positive relationship based on trust, respect, and attentive care enhances your parrot's well-being and promotes a harmonious companionship that enriches both your lives.

7.3 Tips for Creating a Stimulating Environment for Pionus Parrots

Creating a stimulating environment is essential for the health, happiness, and overall well-being of Pionus parrots. A stimulating environment promotes mental enrichment, encourages natural behaviors, and prevents boredom, thereby supporting a fulfilling life for your feathered companion. Here's a comprehensive guide to creating a stimulating environment for Pionus parrots:

Importance of a Stimulating Environment

1. Mental Stimulation:

i. A stimulating environment challenges your Pionus parrot's cognitive abilities, encouraging problem-solving skills and preventing boredom.

ii. It promotes mental agility and reduces the risk of behavioral issues associated with stress or lack of mental stimulation.

2. Physical Exercise:

i. Engaging activities and ample space for movement support physical health and fitness in Pionus parrots.

ii. Physical exercise helps prevent obesity, strengthens muscles, and promotes overall physical well-being.

3. Emotional Well-being:

i. A stimulating environment fulfills your parrot's social and psychological needs, enhancing emotional health and reducing stress.

ii. It supports a positive mood and fosters a sense of security and contentment.

Tips for Creating a Stimulating Environment

1. Cage Setup and Layout:

i. Size and Space: Provide a spacious cage that allows room for movement, stretching wings, and exploration.

ii. Perches and Platforms: Include a variety of perches at different heights and textures to promote exercise and prevent foot problems.

iii. Toys and Enrichment: Place toys, swings, and interactive objects throughout the cage to encourage exploration and mental stimulation.

2. Toy Variety and Rotation:

i. Interactive Toys: Offer toys that encourage manipulation, problem-solving, and foraging behaviors, such as puzzle feeders or treat-dispensing toys.

ii. Chewable Items: Provide bird-safe chew toys made from natural materials like untreated wood or vegetable dyes to satisfy chewing instincts.

iii. Rotate Toys Regularly: Change toys and rearrange the cage layout periodically to maintain novelty and prevent habituation.

3. Foraging Opportunities:

i. Foraging Toys: Use foraging toys that require your parrot to work for treats or food, stimulating natural foraging behaviors.

ii. Scatter Feeding: Scatter food or treats in different areas of the cage or play area to encourage active foraging and exploration.

4. Social Interaction:

i. Human Interaction: Spend quality time interacting with your parrot daily through talking, training sessions, or gentle handling to promote socialization and bonding.

ii. Companion Birds: Consider providing opportunities for social interaction with compatible companion parrots if appropriate for your Pionus.

5. Environmental Enrichment:

i. Natural Elements: Introduce natural elements such as branches, leaves, or safe plants (non-toxic) to mimic the parrot's natural habitat and provide sensory stimulation.

ii. Visual and Auditory Stimulation: Place the cage in a location with views of natural light, outdoor scenery, or household activities for visual and auditory enrichment.

6. Routine and Predictability:

i. Consistent Schedule: Establish a daily routine for feeding, playtime, and social interaction to provide structure and predictability for your parrot.

ii. Enrichment Sessions: Incorporate scheduled enrichment sessions, such as training exercises or interactive play, to stimulate mental and physical activity.

7. Safe and Stimulating Out-of-Cage Time:

i. Supervised Exploration: Allow supervised out-of-cage time in a bird-proofed area to encourage physical exercise, exploration, and social interaction.

ii. Training and Play: Use out-of-cage time for training sessions, flying exercises (if safe and appropriate), and bonding activities to further enrich your parrot's environment.

Monitoring and Adjustment

1. Observation: Regularly observe your parrot's behavior, appetite, and physical condition for signs of boredom, stress, or health issues.

2. Behavior Cues: Recognize behavior cues indicating contentment, curiosity, stress, or discomfort to adjust the environment accordingly.

3. Flexibility and Adaptation: Be flexible in adjusting enrichment activities and the environment based on your parrot's preferences, age, health, and individual personality traits.

Creating a stimulating environment for your Pionus parrot is fundamental to their overall health, happiness, and quality of life. By providing a diverse range of toys, opportunities for mental and physical exercise, social interaction, and environmental enrichment, you can meet their natural needs and foster a fulfilling life. Regularly assess and adjust the environment based on your parrot's responses and evolving needs to ensure ongoing stimulation and well-being. With thoughtful planning and attention to their individual preferences, you can create a dynamic and enriching environment that supports a thriving companionship with your Pionus parrot.

CHAPTER EIGHT

Breeding and Reproduction

8.1 Overview of Pionus Parrot Breeding

Breeding Pionus parrots can be a rewarding but challenging endeavor that requires careful planning, knowledge of avian behavior, and dedication to the welfare of both parent birds and offspring. Here's a comprehensive overview of Pionus parrot breeding:

Understanding Pionus Parrot Breeding Behavior

1. Breeding Season:

Pionus parrots typically breed during specific seasons, often in response to environmental cues such as changes in daylight or temperature. Depending on the species, breeding seasons may vary, but they generally occur during spring and early summer in their native habitats.

2. Pair Bonding:

Pionus parrots form strong pair bonds, often remaining monogamous throughout the breeding season. Bonding rituals include mutual preening, courtship displays, and vocalizations to establish and maintain their partnership.

3. Nesting Behavior:

In the wild, Pionus parrots nest in tree cavities, using bark, leaves, and other plant materials to construct their nests. In captivity, providing a suitable nesting box or cavity mimicking natural conditions is crucial for successful breeding.

Preparation for Breeding

1. Health Assessment:

i. Ensure both potential breeding pairs are in optimal health, free from infections, parasites, or nutritional deficiencies.

ii. Schedule a pre-breeding health check with an avian veterinarian to evaluate reproductive readiness and overall wellness.

2. Diet and Nutrition:

i. Provide a balanced and nutritious diet rich in fresh fruits, vegetables, high-quality pellets, and occasional supplements such as calcium and vitamins.

ii. Adjust diet and supplements to support breeding conditions and egg production, ensuring adequate nutrition for parent birds and chicks.

3. Nesting Environment:

i. Select a suitable nesting box or cavity with dimensions appropriate for the species, lined with clean, non-toxic bedding material.

ii. Ensure the nesting area is placed in a quiet, secure location within the aviary or breeding enclosure to minimize disturbances.

Breeding and Incubation

1. Egg Laying and Incubation:

i. Female Pionus parrots typically lay a clutch of 2-4 eggs, with incubation lasting approximately 25-28 days.

ii. Both male and female birds share incubation duties, taking turns to maintain optimal temperature and humidity levels.

2. Chick Development:

i. Chicks hatch naked and helpless, relying on parental care for warmth, feeding, and protection.

ii. Parent birds regurgitate food to feed the chicks, gradually introducing solid foods as they mature.

Challenges and Considerations

1. Behavioral Monitoring:

i. Monitor breeding pairs closely for signs of aggression, abandonment, or inadequate parental care.

ii. Be prepared to intervene if necessary, providing supplementary feeding or fostering chicks if parental care is insufficient.

2. Health and Veterinary Care:

i. Schedule regular check-ups for breeding pairs and chicks with an avian veterinarian to monitor health, growth, and development.

ii. Address any health concerns promptly, including infections, nutritional deficiencies, or developmental issues.

Ethical Considerations

1. Responsible Breeding Practices:

i. Practice responsible breeding ethics, prioritizing the health and welfare of parent birds and offspring.

ii. Avoid overbreeding and ensure proper placement of chicks in knowledgeable and caring homes.

2. Conservation Efforts:

i. Consider participating in conservation programs or initiatives that support the preservation of Pionus parrot species in their natural habitats.

ii. Educate others about responsible pet ownership and conservation efforts to protect wild populations.

Breeding Pionus parrots requires thorough preparation, understanding of avian behavior, and commitment to ethical practices. By providing a suitable nesting environment, monitoring reproductive health, and supporting parental care, breeders can contribute to the preservation and welfare of these fascinating avian species. Responsible breeding practices ensure the well-being of parent birds and offspring, fostering a positive impact on conservation efforts and promoting the enjoyment of these intelligent and charming parrots as companions.

8.2 Nesting Requirements and Breeding Season of Pionus Parrots

Understanding nesting requirements and the breeding season of Pionus parrots is essential for successfully facilitating breeding and ensuring the well-being of both parent birds and offspring. Here's a comprehensive overview:

Nesting Requirements

1. Nesting Boxes or Cavities:

i. Pionus parrots prefer nesting in enclosed spaces that simulate tree cavities found in their natural habitat.

ii. Provide nesting boxes or cavities made from wood, with dimensions suitable for the specific species of Pionus parrot.

2. Size and Placement:

i. Select a nesting box with dimensions appropriate for the species, typically ranging from 10x10x12 inches for smaller species to larger dimensions for larger species like the Blue-headed Pionus.

ii. Place the nesting box in a quiet, secure location within the aviary or breeding enclosure, ensuring privacy and minimizing disturbances.

3. Bedding Material:

i. Line the nesting box with clean, non-toxic bedding material such as untreated wood shavings or shredded paper.

ii. Avoid using materials that may harbor mold or bacteria, ensuring a hygienic environment for egg incubation and chick rearing.

4. Natural Environment Simulation:

i. Mimic natural nesting conditions by providing materials such as bark, leaves, or pine needles inside the nesting box.

ii. These materials encourage nesting behavior and provide insulation and comfort for parent birds and developing chicks.

Breeding Season

1. Seasonal Cues:

i. Pionus parrots typically breed in response to seasonal cues such as changes in daylight hours and temperature.

ii. Breeding season varies among species and geographical regions but often occurs during spring and early summer.

2. Courtship and Pair Bonding:

i. During the breeding season, Pionus parrots engage in courtship rituals that strengthen pair bonds.

ii. Courtship behaviors include mutual preening, vocalizations, and displays of affection to establish and maintain their relationship.

3. Egg Laying and Incubation:

i. Female Pionus parrots lay a clutch of 2-4 eggs, typically one egg every other day.

ii. Both male and female birds share incubation duties, taking turns to maintain optimal temperature and humidity within the nesting box.

4. Chick Rearing:

i. Chicks hatch approximately 25-28 days after incubation begins, initially relying on parental care for warmth, protection, and feeding.

ii. Parent birds regurgitate food to feed the chicks, gradually introducing solid foods as they mature.

Monitoring and Care

1. Observational Monitoring:

i. Monitor breeding pairs closely for signs of egg laying, incubation progress, and chick development.

ii. Observe parental behavior for signs of adequate care, feeding, and protection of offspring.

2. Health and Nutrition:

i. Ensure breeding pairs receive a balanced diet rich in nutrients, vitamins, and minerals to support reproductive health and egg production.

ii. Provide supplementary foods such as calcium sources for female birds during egg laying to prevent nutritional deficiencies.

3. Veterinary Care:

i. Schedule regular health check-ups for breeding pairs and chicks with an avian veterinarian to monitor health, growth, and development.

ii. Address any health concerns promptly, including infections, parasites, or developmental issues that may affect breeding success.

Nesting requirements and understanding the breeding season of Pionus parrots are crucial for fostering successful breeding outcomes and ensuring the welfare of these intelligent and charismatic birds. By providing suitable nesting boxes or cavities, mimicking natural nesting conditions, and monitoring seasonal breeding cues, breeders can support healthy reproduction and chick development. Responsible breeding practices, including veterinary care, nutrition, and ethical considerations, contribute to the conservation and enjoyment of Pionus parrots as companions while promoting their well-being in captivity and conservation efforts in the wild.

8.3 Caring for Breeding Pairs and Chicks of Pionus Parrots

Caring for breeding pairs and chicks of Pionus parrots requires dedicated attention to their health, nutritional needs, environmental conditions, and behavioral well-being. Successful breeding and chick rearing depend on providing optimal care throughout the breeding process. Here's a comprehensive guide:

Preparing for Breeding

1. Health Assessment:

i. Before breeding, ensure both parent birds are in optimal health with regular veterinary check-ups.

ii. Address any health concerns, infections, or nutritional deficiencies that may affect breeding success.

2. Nesting Environment:

i. Provide a suitable nesting box or cavity lined with clean, non-toxic bedding material.

ii. Place the nesting area in a quiet, secure location within the aviary to minimize disturbances and ensure privacy.

3. Nutrition and Diet:

i. Offer a balanced diet rich in fresh fruits, vegetables, high-quality pellets, and occasional supplements such as calcium and vitamins.

ii. Adjust the diet to support reproductive health, egg production, and chick development, providing additional nutrients as needed.

During Breeding

1. Monitoring Behavior:

i. Observe breeding pairs for courtship behavior, egg laying, and incubation progress.

ii. Ensure both male and female birds are actively involved in incubation duties and caring for eggs.

2. Incubation and Egg Care:

i. Monitor temperature and humidity levels within the nesting box to maintain optimal conditions for egg development.

ii. Avoid disturbing the nesting area unnecessarily to minimize stress on parent birds and eggs.

3. Providing Support:

i. Offer supplementary foods and treats to support parental nutrition and egg laying, including calcium-rich foods for females.

ii. Provide access to clean water and ensure both parent birds have easy access to food during the breeding process.

Caring for Chicks

1. Hatchling Care:

i. Monitor chicks closely after hatching for signs of health, including proper feeding and warmth.

ii. Ensure parent birds are feeding chicks regularly and providing adequate warmth and protection.

2. Feeding and Nutrition:

i. Parent birds regurgitate food to feed chicks initially, gradually introducing solid foods as chicks mature.

ii. Supplement the diet with appropriate foods for chicks, ensuring they receive essential nutrients for growth and development.

3. Environmental Conditions:

i. Maintain stable environmental conditions, including temperature and humidity levels, to support chick health and growth.

ii. Provide a clean and safe environment free from drafts or temperature fluctuations that could compromise chick well-being.

Behavioral Observation and Interaction

1. Bonding and Socialization:

i. Foster bonding between parent birds and chicks through positive interactions and attentive care.

ii. Avoid unnecessary handling or disturbances that may cause stress to parent birds or chicks during critical developmental stages.

2. Behavioral Monitoring:

i. Monitor chick behavior for signs of health, growth milestones, and developmental progress.

ii. Observe parent birds for continued care and behavior adjustments as chicks grow and become more independent.

Veterinary Care and Health Monitoring

1. Regular Check-ups:

i. Schedule regular veterinary check-ups for breeding pairs and chicks to monitor health, growth, and development.

ii. Address any health concerns promptly, including infections, nutritional deficiencies, or developmental issues.

2. Emergency Preparedness:

i. Be prepared to intervene if necessary, providing supplemental feeding, hand-rearing assistance, or medical care under veterinary guidance.

ii. Have a plan in place for emergencies, including contact information for an avian veterinarian experienced in treating Pionus parrots.

Caring for breeding pairs and chicks of Pionus parrots requires meticulous attention to their physical health, nutritional needs, environmental conditions, and behavioral well-being throughout the breeding process. By providing a supportive nesting environment, monitoring breeding behaviors, and ensuring optimal nutrition and veterinary care, breeders can contribute to successful reproduction and the welfare of these captivating avian species. Responsible breeding practices and ethical considerations play a crucial role in promoting the conservation and enjoyment of Pionus parrots as companions while supporting efforts to preserve their natural habitats and wild populations.

CHAPTER NINE

Advanced Care and Expert Tips

9.1 Advanced Training Techniques for Pionus Parrots

Advanced training techniques for Pionus parrots go beyond basic commands and behaviors, focusing on enhancing cognitive abilities, fostering complex skills, and strengthening the bond between parrot and owner. These techniques require patience, consistency, and an understanding of avian behavior. Here's a comprehensive guide to advanced training techniques for Pionus parrots:

Foundation and Preparation

1. Establish Trust and Bonding:

Before beginning advanced training, establish a strong bond of trust with your Pionus parrot through positive interactions, respect for their cues, and consistent rewards. Ensure your parrot is comfortable with basic commands and handling to build a foundation for more complex training tasks.

2. Create a Positive Learning Environment:

Choose a quiet, distraction-free area for training sessions where your parrot feels safe and focused. Use positive reinforcement techniques, such as treats, praise, or favorite toys, to motivate and reward desired behaviors.

Advanced Training Techniques

1. Target Training:

i. Teach your Pionus parrot to target a specific object, such as a stick or your finger, by touching it with their beak.

ii. Expand target training to include targeting to different locations or objects, fostering problem-solving and directional skills.

2. Recall Training:

i. Train your parrot to come to you on command by using a consistent recall cue paired with positive reinforcement.

ii. Gradually increase distance and distractions during recall training sessions to strengthen their responsiveness.

3. Vocalization and Mimicry:

i. Encourage vocalization and mimicry by teaching your parrot specific words, phrases, or sounds through repetition and positive reinforcement.

ii. Use mimicry training to engage your parrot in interactive conversations or responses to cues and environmental stimuli.

4. Complex Behaviors:

i. Teach complex behaviors such as retrieving objects, opening and closing containers, or sorting colors using progressive training steps.

ii. Break down tasks into smaller achievable goals, reinforcing each step with rewards to build confidence and motivation.

5. Problem-Solving Skills:

i. Provide enrichment activities and puzzles that challenge your parrot's problem-solving abilities, such as foraging toys or interactive games.

ii. Rotate toys and activities regularly to maintain novelty and mental stimulation, promoting cognitive development.

Advanced Behavioral Training

1. Desensitization and Counterconditioning:

i. Use desensitization techniques to gradually introduce your parrot to feared or stressful stimuli, pairing each exposure with positive experiences.

ii. Counterconditioning involves replacing negative associations with positive ones to change your parrot's emotional response.

2. Agility and Flight Training:

i. Incorporate agility training by setting up obstacle courses or perches of varying heights and distances for your parrot to navigate.

ii. Practice flight training in a safe, controlled environment to enhance wing strength, coordination, and confidence in flight.

Monitoring Progress and Challenges

1. Regular Assessment:

i. Monitor your parrot's progress in advanced training tasks, noting improvements, setbacks, and areas for further development.

ii. Adjust training methods as needed based on your parrot's responses, preferences, and learning pace.

2. Patience and Consistency:

i. Remain patient and consistent in your training efforts, acknowledging that learning complex behaviors takes time and repetition.

ii. Avoid rushing or forcing your parrot into tasks they find stressful, adapting training sessions to maintain a positive learning experience.

Advanced training techniques for Pionus parrots enhance their cognitive abilities, promote physical agility, and deepen the bond between parrot and owner. By establishing a foundation of trust, creating a positive learning environment, and using progressive training methods, owners can nurture their parrot's intelligence and skills while fostering a rewarding companionship. Advanced training encourages mental stimulation, problem-solving, and behavioral flexibility, enriching the lives of Pionus parrots and strengthening the human-parrot relationship through mutual respect and understanding.

9.2 Nutrition Adjustments for Breeding or Senior Parrots

Nutrition adjustments for breeding or senior Pionus parrots are crucial to support their specific physiological needs during different life stages. Proper nutrition plays a vital role in maintaining overall health, reproductive success, and longevity. Here's a comprehensive guide to nutrition adjustments for breeding or senior Pionus parrots:

Breeding Parrots

1. Increased Caloric Needs:

During the breeding season, female parrots require increased calories to support egg production, incubation, and chick feeding. Provide a balanced diet with slightly higher fat and protein content to meet the energy demands of breeding.

2. Calcium Supplementation:

Female parrots may benefit from additional calcium sources to support eggshell formation and prevent calcium depletion. Offer calcium-rich foods such as cuttlebone, calcium blocks, or leafy greens like kale and broccoli.

3. Fresh Foods and Nutritional Variety:

Incorporate fresh fruits, vegetables, and sprouted seeds into their diet to provide essential vitamins, minerals, and antioxidants. Rotate food items regularly to ensure nutritional variety and prevent monotony in their diet.

4. Protein-Rich Foods:

Include protein-rich foods such as cooked beans, legumes, and lean meats (in moderation) to support muscle development and reproductive health. Avoid feeding high-fat or processed foods that may contribute to obesity or metabolic imbalances.

5. Hydration:

Ensure breeding parrots have access to clean, fresh water at all times to support egg production, digestion, and overall hydration.

Senior Parrots

1. Reduced Caloric Needs:

i. Senior parrots may have decreased activity levels and metabolic rate, requiring fewer calories to maintain a healthy weight.

ii. Adjust portion sizes and food offerings accordingly to prevent obesity and related health issues.

2. Digestive Health:

i. Monitor digestive health and offer easily digestible foods such as cooked grains, soft fruits, and vegetables to support gastrointestinal function.

ii. Provide access to probiotics or digestive enzymes under veterinary guidance to promote gut health and nutrient absorption.

3. Joint and Muscle Support:

i. Incorporate foods rich in omega-3 fatty acids, such as flaxseeds or oily fish (like salmon), to support joint health and reduce inflammation.

ii. Offer foods with natural antioxidants (e.g., berries, sweet potatoes) to support immune function and overall vitality.

4. Vitamin and Mineral Supplements:

i. Consider supplementation with vitamins (especially Vitamin D3) and minerals to address deficiencies common in senior parrots, based on veterinary recommendations.

ii. Avoid over-supplementation and monitor blood levels to prevent imbalances or toxicity.

5. Fresh Water and Hydration:

Ensure senior parrots have access to clean, fresh water at all times to support kidney function, hydration, and overall health.

General Considerations

1. Regular Veterinary Check-ups:

i. Schedule regular check-ups with an avian veterinarian to monitor nutritional needs, health status, and any age-related conditions.

ii. Discuss dietary adjustments and supplementation based on individual health assessments and blood work results.

2. Monitoring Body Condition:

i. Monitor body condition scores regularly to assess weight management and nutritional adequacy.

ii. Adjust diet and feeding practices based on changes in activity levels, health conditions, or seasonal variations.

3. Environmental Factors:

i. Consider environmental factors such as temperature, humidity, and seasonal changes that may affect appetite, metabolism, and nutritional requirements.

ii. Provide a stable and comfortable environment that promotes physical activity, mental stimulation, and social interaction.

Nutrition adjustments for breeding or senior Pionus parrots are essential to support their specific physiological needs, promote reproductive health, and ensure longevity and quality of life. By providing a balanced diet with appropriate caloric intake, essential nutrients, and supplemental support as needed, owners can optimize their parrot's health during different life stages. Regular veterinary care, monitoring of body condition, and environmental considerations further contribute to the overall well-being and vitality of breeding or senior Pionus parrots, fostering a healthy and enriching companionship for years to come.

9.3 Long-term Care and Lifespan Considerations for Pionus Parrots

Long-term care and lifespan considerations are crucial aspects of responsible ownership for Pionus parrots. Providing proper care throughout their lives ensures their health, well-being, and longevity. Here's a comprehensive guide to long-term care and lifespan considerations for Pionus parrots:

Understanding Lifespan

1. Lifespan Variability:

Pionus parrots have a lifespan that varies depending on species, genetics, diet, environment, and overall care. On average, they can live between 25 to 40 years in captivity, with proper care potentially extending their lifespan.

2. Species-specific Considerations:

Research and understand the specific lifespan expectations and care requirements for the species of Pionus parrot you own. Factors such as size, diet, and genetic predispositions can influence their longevity and health outcomes.

Providing Proper Nutrition

1. Balanced Diet:

Offer a varied diet consisting of high-quality pellets, fresh fruits, vegetables, nuts, and seeds to meet their nutritional needs. Monitor portion sizes and adjust feeding practices based on age, activity levels, and health conditions to prevent obesity or malnutrition.

2. Hydration:

Ensure access to clean, fresh water at all times to support digestion, hydration, and overall health. Monitor water consumption and cleanliness of water containers regularly.

Veterinary Care

1. Regular Check-ups:

Schedule annual wellness exams with an avian veterinarian to monitor overall health, detect early signs of illness, and discuss preventative care. Senior parrots may require more frequent check-ups to monitor age-related conditions such as arthritis or heart disease.

2. Diagnostic Testing:

Consider diagnostic testing such as blood work, fecal exams, and imaging studies to assess internal health, nutritional status, and early detection of diseases. Discuss vaccination protocols and parasite prevention strategies with your veterinarian.

Environmental Enrichment

1. Mental Stimulation:

Provide mental enrichment through toys, puzzles, foraging activities, and social interaction to prevent boredom and promote cognitive health. Rotate toys regularly and create an engaging environment that encourages natural behaviors.

2. Physical Exercise:

Encourage physical activity through supervised playtime, flight exercises (if appropriate), and access to perches of varying sizes and textures. Promote natural behaviors such as climbing, chewing, and exploration to maintain muscle tone and mental agility.

Social Interaction and Bonding

1. Bonding Opportunities:

Foster a strong bond through positive reinforcement, interactive play, and consistent training sessions that build trust and communication. Spend quality time with your parrot daily to strengthen the bond and provide companionship.

2. Socialization:

Introduce your parrot to new people, environments, and experiences gradually to reduce fear and promote socialization skills. Monitor social interactions with other pets or household members to ensure safety and comfort for your parrot.

Age-related Care Considerations

1. Mobility and Comfort:

Provide ergonomic perches, ramps, or platforms to support joint health and ease of movement, especially for senior parrots and monitor for signs of arthritis, stiffness, or mobility issues and adjust the environment as needed for comfort.

2. Nutritional Adjustments:

Modify diet and supplementation based on age-related changes in metabolism, digestive efficiency, and nutrient absorption and offer softer foods or nutritional supplements to address dental health and ensure adequate nutrient intake.

End-of-Life Considerations

1. Palliative Care:

Provide compassionate care, pain management, and supportive measures for parrots experiencing age-related illnesses or declining health. Consult with your veterinarian to discuss quality of life assessments and consider humane end-of-life decisions when necessary.

2. Bereavement Support:

Seek support from avian veterinarians or pet loss counselors to cope with the emotional impact of losing a beloved parrot companion. Honor their memory through remembrance rituals or creating a legacy that celebrates their life and impact on your family.

Long-term care and lifespan considerations for Pionus parrots involve providing a nurturing environment, proper nutrition, veterinary care, enrichment activities, and social interaction throughout their lives. By prioritizing their physical health, mental well-being, and emotional bond with their human caregivers, owners can enhance the quality of life and longevity of their parrot companions. Responsible ownership includes adapting care practices based on age-related changes and embracing the role of stewardship in providing a fulfilling and enriched life for Pionus parrots from their youth through their golden years.

__Thanks For Reading!__

Made in United States
Troutdale, OR
04/30/2025

31014928R00076